GROWING UP DEAD

GROWING UP DEAD

BRENDA RABKIN

McClelland and Stewart

The Canadian Publishers
McClelland and Stewart Limited
25 Hollinger Road
Toronto M4B 3G2

Canadian Cataloguing in Publication Data

Rabkin, Brenda.
  Growing up dead

ISBN 0-7710-7230-9

1. Youth—Suicidal behavior.   2. Suicide.
I. Title.

HV6546.R32   364.1'522   C78-001227-5

Manufactured in Canada by Webcom Limited

CONTENTS

ACKNOWLEDGEMENTS

I wish to acknowledge the Explorations Program of the Canada Council for their support, and *Homemaker's* magazine for their indispensable co-operation. I would also like to acknowledge Dr. Herbert Hendin, whose book, *The Age of Sensation*, is the source for the title "Growing Up Dead". I must thank Simon, Jessica, Abby, and Andy for their unfailing love and encouragement. And most important, I wish to thank all those young people who so courageously shared their pain, so that others could learn and take hope.

Special thanks to Jean Chatterson, without whose inspiration this book would never have been written.

Brenda Rabkin
Winnipeg, 1978

PREFACE

You, the potential reader, may well be thinking, "Not another book on suicide!" To this I must quickly answer, "Yes, and a very important one!" Brenda Rabkin has succeeded in combining the pathos, the intensity, and the individuality of the adolescents, with the scientific, the clinical, and the philosophical. Few others have attempted this difficult task, and certainly nobody else, in my experience, has succeeded with such impact.

When I read this book, I experienced two central feelings – poignancy and hope. Ms. Rabkin has a way of getting young people to reveal their innermost sufferings and yearnings to her, and she handles them sensitively and delicately. The adolescents tell their own stories, and the reader can experience some of the pain and futility that they felt at crucial times in their lives. The adolescents who talk to us represent the spectrum of psychological and social backgrounds and problems. There is no single type of suicidal adolescent.

Ms. Rabkin describes and delves into the phenomenon of adolescent suicide with seriousness. She is not, however, alarmist or melodramatic. She tells us what is known and what is not known, and she debunks myths and popularly held but invalid misconceptions. We learn that there are few real "experts" in the field, but many self-styled pontificators. We learn that it is not a subject for psychiatrists alone, that it has equally relevant philosophical and social ramifications.

We also learn that much can be done both on the social level and individually to prevent young people from killing themselves. Ms. Rabkin pulls no punches: she is critical of some mental health professionals whose approaches to adolescents and their problems are either atavistic or destructive. She points out the problems in our society that affect our youth, and discusses how we – society – have failed them.

But she is not simplistic. No group is singled out as solely responsible for a tragic situation. In reviewing the literature on the subject, the author shows us just how muddled and complicated a subject this is. Paradoxically, she discovers that for all the heat, there is little light. For all the rhetoric and emotions raised, there are relatively few accurate statements that can be made about aetiology, causality, intervention, and prevention. Accompanied by the young people with whom she talked, and with the experts' pronouncements, we become confused, skeptical, and moderately pessimistic.

Subtly, Ms. Rabkin leads us from there to a feeling of optimism. There *are* some facts we can rely on. There *are* ways of reaching adolescents in trouble. Many of the young people who made attempts on their lives were grateful that they had not succeeded.

Ms. Rabkin has written an inspiring book that must be read by adolescents, their parents, and the professionals involved with them. Her thinking is clear and cogent, her style moving and exciting. *Growing Up Dead* informs, it teaches, but most importantly, it helps.

Saul V. Levine, M.D., C.M., F.R.C.P.(C)
Senior Psychiatrist, Hospital for Sick Children, Toronto
Professor, Department of Psychiatry, University of Toronto

INTRODUCTION

Two years ago I came across a tiny paragraph in the news-paper. It simply stated that adolescent suicide had tripled in the past twenty years. This information aroused my interest immediately. It had never really occurred to me that young people *did* that. True, I had read of the odd account of a young person who had died as a result of a drug overdose, and suicide was implied, though hard to prove. Then I remembered those Indian youths in Ontario who had killed themselves in order to rejoin their tribal ancestors; but that was part of their culture. But that self-inflicted death among young people was a reality and was being reported as coolly as the annual snowfall – I didn't know what to make of it, but I was troubled. Why do young people who have their whole lives ahead of them do away with themselves? What kinds of kids do it? How do they do it? Do they calmly put guns to their heads? Do they slash their wrists? And what role do drugs play? Is there anything we can do to stop it?

The more I thought about it, the more curious I became. Clearly, suicide fascinated me as much as it horrified me, and I wanted to find out more about it. I also felt that, as a parent, perhaps there was something I should know, because my small daughter would one day grow up to be an adolescent. So with a mixture of scientific detachment and somewhat ghoulish de-sire for detail I went to the university library, hoping to find the answers to my questions.

What I found was a voluminous and rapidly increasing out-put on the subject of suicide; it had even been designated as a separate field of study, appropriately called suicidology. There were countless articles, monographs and textbooks dealing with suicide. Suicide intent was charted and plotted on graphs. Its frequency was mapped out in demographic studies. The symp-toms of suicide were described again and again, and were as vague and all-encompassing as horoscopes. So, too, with the causes of suicide, which ranged from family breakdown to urbanization, to depression, to hopelessness, all duly laid out in neat tables. To make matters worse, the literature was comprised of such elaborate jargon and convoluted syntax that I felt like an archaeologist cutting through layers of debris in order to discover a few precious artifacts. Like the archaeologist, I found my artifacts, but mine revealed nothing about the people they were supposed to represent.

I wanted to understand why the social scientists studied it so assiduously. My experience as a broadcast journalist made me decide two things: First, I wanted to talk to kids who had tried it, and perhaps to parents of kids who had tried it, both successfully and unsuccessfully, because in radio and television, everything possible is actuality. (The philosophy is that the viewer or listener must witness the act, or it's not real.) Second, whatever my findings, I wanted to share them with an audience. Surely a subject that was so inherently a part of the life process and which had generated so much scientific literature over the years was worthy of some public attention. I chose radio as the medium, because it afforded the most intimacy and anonymity, both of which were crucial to a discussion of the subject.

I approached two prominent psychiatrists in the hope that they would help me find young people to talk to. One categorically refused on the grounds that any publicity would surely prompt a rash of further suicides. As if to give authority to his argument, he assured me that the contagion theory of suicide was widely accepted. The other psychiatrist thought that my project was essential, and agreed to help; but he must have changed his mind, as he studiously avoided my many phone calls and messages. The director of the city's only drop-in centre, which serviced hundreds of young people a month, also refused to help for reasons so vague I can no longer recall them.

It was becoming painfully apparent that suicide was a subject that people were not going to discuss readily. This reticence, I was later to discover, characterizes our whole attitude to suicide. We fear it; we abhor it. Some of us are attracted to it, perhaps as an act in itself, perhaps as a solution to life's problems; some of us who have had a close relationship with a

10

suicide victim may feel guilty, because we may feel partly responsible for his death. This is true of professionals as well, to whom the loss of a patient through suicide must surely represent a personal as well as a professional failure, and may explain their reluctance to discuss the subject. Suicide is not a topic we're comfortable with.

That I finally found people who were willing to discuss their suicide attempts with me – honestly and with introspection – was due to fortuitous circumstance on my part, and a good deal of courage on theirs. Almost everyone I interviewed wanted to share their experiences, so others could learn from their pain, and perhaps find some insights and comforts for their own. As one eighteen-year-old put it, "I want to reach out to people now, the way others reached out to me when I needed it."

The radio documentary was completed and aired, and I later followed it with a magazine article. The response to both overwhelmed me. Hundreds of letters poured in from kids saying that they were able for the first time to open up a discussion with their parents. They didn't feel like emotional freaks anymore, knowing now that other kids shared their problems and feelings. Parents wrote in for similar reasons. Teachers, psychologists, and social workers asked for permission to use the material for instructional seminars. All those who responded stressed the need for the subject of adolescent suicide to be dealt with openly and rationally, and in a manner that everyone could understand and relate to. They were both grateful and relieved. The attempts to reach out had been well received, and had been proven necessary.

That is why I wrote this book. It's an attempt to present suicide not as a science, but as a human expression, from the point of view, and indeed in the very words, of people who have experienced it.

What then are the causes of adolescent suicide? Why do young people kill themselves? It is very easy to speculate on the causes of suicide among young people, but it is precisely this easy speculation that makes it very difficult to build a case against suicide. If life is such a mess, if no one in our family cares about us and society cares less; if there is no God that we can relate to; if we feel cut off from the past or the future, and the present is painful at worst or meaningless at best, then isn't suicide a reasonable solution? Why should we cope? And is coping really better than not coping?

To say that one ought not to commit suicide because life is sacred is annoyingly facile and unconvincing. We need only look at history, and more recently, at our own twentieth century, to know that it is not. To talk about religious or moral prohibitions is equally unsatisfying because they don't have meaning to many people. Why then should we bother?

It is comforting to consider Camus' Sisyphus struggling with all his might to push that rock up the steep hill. That he knows that it will roll down again as soon as he has pushed it to the top is incidental. Sisyphus earns his dignity from his struggle; he defines himself through it. It's tempting to think that his decision to fight for survival is a conscious one. Sisyphus has had to make a choice, and he has chosen life. We respect him for his decision – not because he has chosen life, but because he has opted for the way of life that is most meaningful to him, painful as that way might be. And he sticks to it stubbornly, though he has plenty of opportunity to change his mind. Sisyphus has considered all the possibilities.

The terrible tragedy of adolescent suicide isn't only the end result – death. But the decision to die (if indeed it is a decision and not a sudden impulse) leaves us with tortured and unanswered questions. Did that young person really consider all the possibilities? Did he have enough experience in his short life to know that ending it was what he really wanted? Could he be sure death was best for him? If only he had struggled a bit longer, perhaps he would have seen things differently, we are sure to say. We can respect Sisyphus' decision to live or Hemingway's commitment to die because we assume that both acts were carried out with mature judgement, developed through a lifetime of varied experiences. But how do we accept the suicide of a young person?

The stories in this book are the stories of survivors, of young people who attempted suicide, failed, and later found their own private justifications for living. The exception is Peter Walker, who succeeded, and who left detailed journals and poetry in an attempt to explain his action. The reader will have to decide for himself if Peter was right or true to himself in doing what he did.

If in writing this book I have betrayed a bias towards life, towards coping, I have no rebuttal. The many teenagers in this book – who are its true authors – have demonstrated that, at least for me, such a bias is justified.

I still don't have any of the answers I set out to find; I don't think there are any. The one generalization I can make is that young people commit suicide because of unbearable pain and a conviction that life is without hope, that new tomorrows are just miserable repeats of old yesterdays; so to continue living is pointless. The end often comes impulsively, with little or no planning. Aside from that generality, each act of suicide is as idiosyncratic as the individual committing it. To view suicide solely in terms of theories and statistics is to ignore the human agony that prompts the act.

1

SUICIDE IS EASY

Foolish man, what do you bemoan and what do you fear? Wherever you look there is an end of evils. You see that yawning precipice? It leads to liberty. You see that flood, that river, that well? Liberty houses within them. You see that stunted, parched and sorry tree? From each branch liberty hangs. Your neck, your throat, your heart are all so many ways of escape from slavery ... Do you inquire the road to freedom? You shall find it in every vein of your body.

Seneca, Dialogues, "De Ira," Bk. 3, Chap. 15, Section 4

Bill

If I look pretty good to you now because I'm sharply dressed, don't pay attention. It's a cover-up really, just an exterior. It's because I feel so badly about the Bill that's inside that I have to make the Bill on the outside look good. I started feeling that way four or five years ago; the booze was starting to catch up with me then.

I was born in a house that was fairly well off. Being the only boy I was spoiled. If I wanted a fire truck and Dad said no, I can remember stamping my feet and banging my head

15

against the wall till I got it. I had all the toys that all the other kids didn't have. They'd come to play in my yard. It had to be Bill's toys, Bill's yard, Bill's game, Bill's rules. It's always been that way.

I started boozing at fifteen. Dad always had lots of booze on hand. There was a bar in the basement. I started drinking after school. Mum and Dad would have people over on the week-end or at the cottage. They'd have four or five of these little brown drinks and start laughing. I knew what was going on. In that bottle there was a high. A different feeling. It felt good. A long time prior to this I'd been thinking about drinking. So I came home from school after a bad argument and I tried it. I got high after a couple of belts of rye.

And it felt good. Really good. I said, "Hey, this is all right!" I had no worries. It was neat. Wobbly, but a real lift. After that I was coming home every day from school and drinking. By the time I was eighteen I had friends going to the liquor store and buying me bottles. I was drinking pretty heavily. Dad and Mum never did too much about it. They just said, "Don't drink, it's bad for you." They never did too much about anything I did wrong.

Dad didn't value me as a person. Like I was a football player. A damned good one. I was a lot heavier then than I am now. I enjoyed sports tremendously. Anyway he was always telling me to play football and hockey. So I did. I was a hockey player. I played junior. He never once came out to the arena. Not even for a tournament. I'd say, "Hey, Dad. There's a tournament all day Saturday and Sunday. Please come out." He never came out. Not once. I don't know why. I've never asked him, but I think that some day I will. It really made me feel bad. He would come out to baseball, though. It would be nice out and he could go out in the stands in a short-sleeved shirt. Dad has always been terribly fond of tanning. When we'd get into a huddle I'd always be looking to see if Dad was there.

At first I remember going home and saying, "Dad, we got beat," or "Dad, we won." He'd say, "Oh, good," or "Too bad." Finally there came a time when I didn't even bother telling him what the score was. I'd just go home and say hi and go straight upstairs and start unpacking all my gear. A couple of times he would say, "What was the score, son?" And I'd say, "Who cares anyway? Where were you?" "Well, I had an appointment." "Sure, thanks, Dad." "I told you I was busy. You don't have to get smart about it." "I'm not getting smart. I'm just disappointed, that's all." And he'd say, "I'm sorry. I'll be out next time." "Ya, sure. In another ten years." "Now stop it. That's enough of that." I'd just turn around and stomp off to my room. I'd get really upset.

I remember there was this all-star juvenile hockey tournament. Our team played on Thursday and Friday. On Saturday was the championship. Nobody came. I came home and got drunk. Then I went back. The coach couldn't believe it. I was sitting there with each arm around a girl, screaming, "Whoopee!" I thought I was a big man. Until the arena cop came and grabbed me by the scruff of the neck and threw me out. I was just cursing and swearing.

Dad wanted me to go to college. I was the only boy in the family so he wanted me to carry on the family name in the family tradition. That meant going to the same college he went to, playing ball on the same ball team, getting a B.A. — the whole bit. I didn't want to do that. I was into radio and music, and I was very good at them. So I wanted to get out and do my own thing. Maybe part of the reason I didn't want to go was to hurt him. It was such a tightly knit community: everyone else went and so had their parents, all the right people did all the right things except me.

Well anyway, Dad, he just about hit the roof. He said, "Okay, Bill, that's fine." It was like slamming the door shut. Ever since, the two of us have had nothing to talk about. Not a thing. Mum? Yes, I could phone her now. She'd probably start crying. I think now I'd probably want to call her when I'm doing okay, when I'm straight for a long period of time. I don't think I could phone her now and say things are peachy keen, because she'd know they weren't. When I'm feeling good I'm a totally different person. I laugh a lot. I'm not laughing too much any more. I don't know if there's any possibility of Dad and I getting together. Maybe if I got my B.A. or Ph.D. I think he wants to go to his grave knowing that Bill's got a Ph.D. behind his name on a door someplace. That isn't important to me.

So I did what I wanted to do. Here I was at nineteen travelling all over with a jazz group. All of a sudden I was the big man on stage. Girls galore. That was going so fine for a long, long time. I was ego tripping all over the place. I don't think I had too many friends — In fact, I know now I didn't have too many friends or I don't think I'd be here in this halfway house now.

At about this time I got married. Can you imagine it, at nineteen? I had gotten this girl pregnant and I really thought I was in love with her. I stayed with her for eighteen months, and found out it was just infatuation. I was drinking a lot, blowing my whole pay cheque on booze. At home there was no food in the fridge. And there was a kid, too. It was terrible. I'd have to phone Dad to help us out. It was too much responsibility for me. Things weren't given to me; I had to go out and earn them on my own and I just didn't like that.

When I left I wanted to go back to music. By this time I was wired every day of the week. Everyone was beginning to pick up on the fact that I had a booze problem. Everyone except me. So I couldn't get back into music. Instead I went out west and became a bartender.

In the last two years I've made two suicide attempts when things started getting really rough. The first time, I met a girl by the name of Patty. She was a straight kid from a good home, the works. When I met her I was a member of AA. I was trying to stay dry. At the time I was thinking, "How can such a fantastic girl come into my life? Just a natural, sweet girl." We really jived and fell in love.

I made big plans to get married. I wanted her. I needed her. She was my mummy; she was going to take care of me. But all my plans fell apart. She said, "The two of us had better hold off for a while because you're an alcoholic. I'd have to see you sober for a year or two first." I said, "I can't wait, I just cannot wait that long." I started immediately feeling sorry for myself and I started drinking.

She had said a long time before that if I started drinking she wouldn't have anything to do with me. I started drinking and she didn't want anything to do with me. I was drinking and drinking, and I really really felt bad. I managed to go straight for a day, but I was so depressed. I called her, but she didn't want to talk to me.

Then I went to a doctor's office and got a supply of a really powerful sleeping pill, the kind that just space you out. I had heard about this doctor. There are some in every town; they're real easy. I was dressed well and told him I couldn't sleep. I gave him twenty-five dollars under the table.

I called her and said, "Patty, I can't stand it. I'm going to kill myself. I've got pills." "Come on, Bill," she said. "Don't talk like that." "Look it," I told her, "I'm going to do it. Can I talk to you?" The last four or five days before calling her I'd been so depressed it was incredible. I'd been thinking that I couldn't take it anymore. Even when I was drinking I was depressed. I just sat in a corner all by myself and I said, "I'll show them. They'll be sorry for me." And that's when I called Patty.

She told me to meet her at the park in half an hour. So I thought, "Hey, if I take the pills now by the time I get to the park there'll be just enough time to die." But by the time I took them I didn't care to die. I took them all at once, without even thinking about it. On the spur of the moment I said to myself, "I'm going to do it," and I didn't think about anything else. I just filled a draft glass with water and dumped all the pills down my throat. It happened so quickly.

Mind you, I had gotten the pills in the morning and this was about five in the afternoon. I carried them around all day and said, "I can't do it. I can't do it." And then I called her, thinking the same thing, until I heard her voice on the phone, and then I thought, "Yes, I can do it." I was really spinny. I wanted someone to feel sorry for me. I was really down. I thought I'd never get back on my feet. Now I think that if she had said, "Take them, I don't care," I would have reacted by saying, "Okay, I'll stay sober and show her."

I thought, "I'll get her back. If Patty sees me sick, and if I'm almost dying . . . But I have to get to her in time so that she'll be able to get me to the hospital." And I got to her in time. At the hospital they pumped my stomach. The following day Patty came to see me and said, "I never want to see you again. Not after this." And I said, "Well, I can't blame you." I straightened up after that.

Two months later I moved in with a fine girl; but she had an alcohol problem and she also popped pills, and I was trying to stay dry. And I was, except for a couple of slips, but I was getting into the habit of falling asleep with Valium. I was taking nine or ten pills a day. Just when I was starting to feel better about me I'd join her because I couldn't stand her drunk. If I was half-gassed too I wouldn't notice so much.

One day I got up and I was all fogged up. I didn't remember how many pills I'd taken. It was getting to the point in our thing together that things were starting to get a little rocky. Everything was coming to a head when she said, "Okay, Bill. It's all over." I just turned around and took a taxi to a sleazy hotel. I had about thirty-five Librium on me. I said, "May as well do it now; get it over with." It was a spur of the moment thing. I ordered double ryes and took all the pills. I didn't even think about it. I found myself starting to nod off in the tavern, so I called her at home. She came and got me and took me to a hospital. They gave me this brown stuff to drink and it made me sick. Then they put me in a detox centre and dried me out. And here I am.

Now it's like a last chance. I've got to get myself together. It's common that the alcoholic dies between twenty-five and forty. And I'm getting there. It's kind of scary, so I'm really starting to apply myself now. I don't feel comfortable doing it, but I'm trying. I don't want to die. Not now.

My suicide attempts were just a matter of losing all hope and saying to myself, "I can't handle it." Not "I won't handle it." There's a difference. Damn it! I didn't even care to try.

And my thinking was so fouled up with alcohol and pills, that there was no way out. I was too fogged up.

When I was a kid and I was angry, I was always told to go up to my room and to come back when I was feeling better. I've never learned to deal with anger — even anger against myself. It's only very recently that I've come to recognize that. These are things I have to learn in order to start living again. Now I've got the courage to handle it. Other people gave it to me. It came mostly from counsellors I trust who have become friends, and from this last girl. In her I saw just how bad I could become. I knew the kind of life I was leading was just no good. There have to be other things to do before I die. I just do not want to live this way any more. It's insane.

I'm sick and tired of being sick. Now if all else fails I have plans of heading straight down to skid row and not stopping. I'll pull up a side alley all of my own and sit there until I die. I don't plan on that happening, but I'm saying, if.

From here I go up, hopefully and slowly. This has been a problem in the past. I've always wanted things NOW. If I stomp my feet and bang my head against the wall I'll get my way. That's the old way. I know now that things don't happen overnight. Now I'm starting to feel a little more comfortable with who Bill is. I even wear jeans.

Doreen

Right now I seem so composed and so together that you find it hard to believe that I ever attempted suicide. Well I did, and not that long ago, either. I guess it was just a point in my life where I was sort of depressed and had a lot of things to work out. It was a turning point about a lot of things. There was a lot of conflict with my family. Afterwards I had to sort out what I wanted to do as opposed to what they wanted me to do. When I thought about it, it made me more determined to get things together the way I wanted to, rather than die.

The circumstances around the attempt had to do with a boyfriend of mine that I had been dating for a long time, who my family didn't like and who I was really serious about. My family didn't like him or his family because they felt I was being corrupted by them with evil ideas. Like my family is quite religious.

My folks were really strict and I didn't feel I was allowed any freedom to make choices. Like with my boyfriend. We were members of a youth group that had conferences across the country, and I was never allowed to go to any that were out of town. All my friends were going, but my parents didn't believe in it. That was really bad. I think you have to let a person kind of test their wings. I think if they'd let me do that I'd have been a lot closer to them — if they'd let me talk about what I really thought. But they didn't want to hear what I had to say.

They wanted me to break off with my boyfriend. It wasn't that I was seeing him too much, but they just felt that my seeing him was interfering with their babysitting plan. So in a way I had a lot of responsibility, but when it came to my own choices, they weren't considered. The injustice of it all made me so angry, but I just didn't know how to deal with it, because when I was growing up I was taught to keep my emotions to myself.

The way I was going with all the pressure building up it wasn't long before I made a suicide attempt. What triggered it off was when my family just flatly told me that I couldn't see him anymore, which I thought was ridiculous. Here I was sixteen years old, and they just said, "You can't see him anymore." We'd been having a lot of conflicts at home. I'd been kicked out a few times, and had left by myself a few times; but I'd always come back. And when they did that I just decided that I'd show them and really make them pay. So I took a whole bunch of pain killers, and I really thought I was going to kill myself.

They were my pills prescribed for me because I had a lot of sinus problems. I'd get really severe sinus headaches. I had quite a storehouse of them, because I didn't take them very often. They really wiped you out! So I took a whole bottle full of them. Then I called my boyfriend and I was talking to him, and he started to suspect something. I wouldn't say for sure, but probably I phoned him deliberately, because I don't think I really wanted to die. At the time I just wanted to make my family pay. I was really mad at them. I guess it was about the only thing I could do so that they couldn't control my life at that point – other than to leave. So I was really showing them. It's sort of stupid.

So my boyfriend figured it out. Apparently he phoned his mother and told her, and then he phoned me back and just talked to me over the phone. He found out how many of what I'd taken, that kind of thing. My parents were home at the time, but they weren't aware of what was going on because my bedroom was downstairs.

My boyfriend told his mother, and she and her husband came over to my place, much to my surprise. By this time I was quite groggy. They told my family, and my family took me to the hospital. The people there gave me the stuff to make you throw up; and everybody at the hospital gave me shit, which I thought was really weird. They made an appointment for me with a psychiatrist for the next day. They didn't take the trouble to find out what the matter was then. They figured they'd let the psychiatrist do it.

Anyway, besides giving me shit, they were all really annoyed with me for wasting their time, which made me feel bad. In retrospect, I don't think that reaction was justified. It's

23

a touchy situation. I think for somebody who tries you have to figure out where they're coming from. For somebody who tries a bunch of times as an attention-getting thing, well then the attitude that the hospital showed me is okay because you're not reinforcing it. It depends on what the reasoning for that person is. For me it worked really badly. If I'd gotten to the suicidal point again, I wouldn't have told anybody. They closed off for me the possibility of a hospital being a place to get help. The next time I would have done it properly, so I wouldn't have to go through that again. They didn't know anything about me when they condemned me. They were really sympathetic towards my parents. You know. "Oh, no. Another daughter in here bothering her parents." That was the sort of attitude.

My parents were shocked at first. Nobody will ever talk about it in my family. Matter of fact, I think my mother might not even remember it. I think she's completely blocked it from her mind. At the time I know they talked to their minister and sought some help themselves. But my mother was worried about what the neighbours would think if they actually found out. She really said that!

When I made the suicide attempt I didn't really think about wanting to die. It didn't even occur to me that it could happen until after I did it. Then I got scared. At the time I just had this one purpose – to get back at my parents. I did it so impulsively. And the one thing that triggered it was when they said, "You can't see him anymore."

After my attempt, my parents figured I'd been under a lot of stress, so they just thought I should go to bed early. They didn't really see their involvement in my stress. They felt I was too involved with my boyfriend, which I might have been. But if you ask me, they handled it all wrong. They could have done something before, but not at that point. They just said, "Go to bed because you're under a lot of stress." We didn't talk about it again. They never sat down and had a heart-to-heart talk with me. But I don't know if I would have wanted them to. It really would have opened up a whole new can of worms and I don't know if I would have wanted that. Things had gone too far. We didn't talk about the emotions between us that much. There was so much to be covered there, it really would have been hard.

I think it did make a difference in our relationship. After that we either didn't talk or we quarrelled. I didn't stay around much longer. It was really tense. I left home when I was seventeen. I didn't have much respect for them anymore.

Go into any classroom in any high school or university and ask the following question: is it all right for someone to commit suicide if he wants to? Assuredly, at least half the students will answer yes. That shouldn't be surprising; it's part of their heritage.

It's often more convenient to destroy life than it is to preserve it. To struggle is harder than to give up the struggle. That's where we're at now – the Age of Convenience.

What we have inherited from the hippies and incorporated into our own views is the credo, "Do your own thing." The fulfilment of the individual is paramount. To young people this is especially meaningful, partly because youth is by nature very self-centred, and partly because many see little around them that they want to belong to: family, school, and church have no appeal, so they turn to themselves. If an individual kills himself, his decision can be viewed as an intensely personal act. It's doing your own thing in the extreme. It's the fullest exercise of civil liberties.

Another way that we can view suicide is as a form of euthanasia. If someone is hopelessly ill, wouldn't it be better for him and for all concerned if doctors pulled the plugs on the machines that are sustaining him? Isn't this "mercy killing" and "death with dignity?" If these expressions have become almost clichés, it's only an indication of how deeply this view has already penetrated our frame of reference. The danger lies in using the logic of what might be a valid and humane medical issue to justify a "right to suicide" issue. One fifteen-year-old girl confused them very easily. In a letter to her therapist she wrote, "Suicide is like mercy killing. People pull plugs on people to put them out of their misery. I want to be put out of my misery but no one will do it for me, so I have to do it myself. When you look at it, it seems so logical."

Of course it's a logical argument; that's what makes it so dangerous. But while a terminally ill patient may, indeed, have no chance of recovery and to keep him alive by artificial means may be cruel, a depressed or unhappy person can be helped and can be taught to cope better with his problems. (In fact, that's exactly what happened to the girl quoted above, as we shall see in chapter seven.) Although a person may feel that his suffering will go on forever, that is often not the case. But if he applies the argument of euthanasia to his own situation, he may find it tragically tempting.

Ironically, the ease with which suicide can be justified philosophically only reflects how extreme is the individual's isolation from society. If the hippies talked about doing your own thing, they also reached out to others around them. For many, there was a rediscovery of tribal life; communes sprang up all over the country, and love-ins and be-ins were held everywhere. There was a real concern for humanity that was especially strongly felt in the anti-war movement. Today that commitment seems to have seriously diminished. The self-fulfilment credo may still be there, but the framework to which it belongs and in which it has meaning is gone. Doing your own thing in isolation can be very lonely and very damaging. It is surely no coincidence that in 1974 the suicide rate among people between fifteen and twenty-four was almost double what it was in 1964.[1]

If the subject of popular songs is any indication of social interests, then suicide is clearly earning a place for itself. Elton John wrote "I Think I'm Gonna Kill Myself." He describes a teenager who is having trouble with his family: he can't get the car, he's got to be in by ten o'clock, and he's angry with his parents. He thinks that perhaps he'll kill himself to make a "little headline news on the state of teenage blues." The British rock group, Thin Lizzie, sings a song entitled simply, "Suicide." And the words to the theme song of "M.A.S.H." are very explicit.

> The game of life is hard to play,
> I'm going to lose it any way,
> The losing card I'll some day lay,
> So this is all I have to say . . .
>
> . . .
>
> Suicide is painless,
> It brings on many changes,
> And I can take or leave it if I please.

The desire for self-destruction is made explicit in these songs.

Suicide is also a reason for romanticizing some of its victims and raising them to the status of tragic heroes. Sylvia Plath, Marilyn Monroe, and Freddie Prinze are now first remembered not for their particular talents, but for their final acts. They're viewed as gifted people who offered themselves up as sacrifices to the pains and sorrows of life. They are for us what Werther was for the nineteenth-century Romantics. Goethe's novel, *The Sorrows of Young Werther*, was about a young man who commits suicide because he is swept away by passions that he cannot control. The Romantics worshipped him because he embodied the ideals that they upheld: to die young and tragically, and to suffer for one's art.

It is not that suicide is an accepted, sanctioned, and encouraged phenomenon in our society. There are still grave moral implications involved in taking one's own life, and such implications are certainly not to be regretted. The suicide notes that people leave when they intend to kill themselves reveal the moral dilemma they find themselves in. Almost invariably, they apologize for what they do and try to make others understand the reasons for their actions. Japanese *kamikaze* pilots or Indian widows who practised *suttee* – throwing themselves on their husbands' funeral pyres to atone for their sins and thereby gain for them entry into paradise – would never have

27

thought of leaving such notes. Their deaths were both sanctioned and expected.

While our society doesn't encourage suicide, clear-cut deterrents don't exist either. By contrast, in mediaeval Europe, for example, it was customary to drag the body of a suicide through the streets, to bury him at a crossroads with a stone on his face and a stake in his heart, or to float him downriver in a barrel. Degrading the body was common, for "the suicide was as low as the lowest criminal."[2] Today, in both Canada and the US, suicide is not regarded as a crime. Attempted suicide has not been regarded a crime in Canada since 1973, and in the US only nine states still hold it a felony, though it's a law that's seldom enforced. Though Christianity and Judaism expressly forbid it, their voices are not loudly heard. The legal prohibitions have been removed – and this is surely enlightened – and all that remains are moral objections, but they are not convincing or restraining enough. Suicide has been made easier.

For anyone contemplating suicide, the means are readily available. Guns, drugs, alcohol, and fast cars are effective and widely used. Most young men who kill themselves use guns, while women prefer drugs. Alcohol, as a slow and perhaps unconscious method of suicide, is easy to come by and barely disapproved of. The same is true of fast cars, but in the cases of alcohol and cars it's more difficult to prove that death was intentional. Some people don't even require physical aids to kill themselves; they choose starvation. One young girl said, "I didn't feel that I was worth anything. I had no friends, no one to talk to. I was really depressed. I wanted to kill myself. I had thoughts of taking a knife or pills, but I couldn't. That was suicide and I knew suicide was a sin. So I just stopped eating. I went down from 120 pounds to 80 pounds. I enjoyed suffering for a while. I felt I deserved it because I was bad."[3]

Finally suicide is made easy because death is viewed as unreal. It's difficult for young people to accept death as final when the only experience most of them have with it is from television or movies. Robert Redford may have been killed in *Butch Cassidy and the Sundance Kid*, but he was resurrected for *All the President's Men*. Kojak may face death every week; but he survives it so effortlessly, as if it's a force not to be contended with seriously. Even when television news shows us real death – the gruesome carnage of war, for example – we often don't even flinch. "That can't be real," we say. "It's TV." It's an experience that doesn't touch us. But the suicides of young people do.

The attempts by Doreen and Bill reveal just how easy suicide can be. Both of them had ready access to potentially lethal means and both of them resorted to these means without hesitation and without any anxiety about the moral correctness of what they were doing. Neither of them understood that they could have died as a result, and yet neither really wanted to die.

Doreen is almost a cliché of attempted suicide stories, and we might be inclined not to take her seriously. It's very easy to slough her off as a hysterical girl who overreacts – that's certainly how the hospital staff sees her. But to take that attitude is to ignore her extreme anger and impotence, in that she can barely begin to deal with her enormous problems.

The style in which we cope with our problems is usually one that we learn from our parents. Doreen was taught to keep her emotions to herself. She learned that her parents didn't really want to hear what she had to say, probably because what she had to say was disagreeable and contrary to what they wanted to hear; and they hardly seem the kind of people who can deal well with open confrontations. Consequently, a situation develops where effective communication is impossible.

The messages that come through to Doreen convey to her that she is not a very worthy person. Her parents don't trust her and they don't respect her emotions. Although she is given a lot of responsibility in caring for her brothers, she isn't allowed to make choices that would establish and confirm her in her own right as a young adult. Her parents forbid her to see her boyfriend, a person for whom she has serious feelings. We can understand the anger and resentment she justifiably feels. But she hasn't been taught to deal with her emotions openly and effectively. She can't confront her parents and talk it out because she doesn't know how, and it probably wouldn't work even if she did. That is not the pattern for problem-solving in her household. What she would like to do is control the situation without having to face her parents; she also wants to punish them because they have hurt her. She has a good supply of pills. In a situation like this, suicide is easy – easy to do and an easy way out of the conflict.

Doreen's attempt at suicide is brought about directly as a result of her anger against her parents. She'll show them who's boss by making them feel guilty and sorry about her death. She doesn't really want to die, but she doesn't know how else to change her environment. Without realizing it, she risks her life to bring about those changes. The game she plays is an extremely dangerous one, but she takes all the necessary precautions so that she won't come out the loser. She takes an overdose of pills while her parents are at home, and then calls her boyfriend to let him know what she's done.

It's been estimated that seventy per cent of teenagers who attempt suicide do so when their parents are still in the house. They then usually call someone else to rescue them.[4] It's their way of saying – desperately – "I am unhappy. I want you to care for me and love me and respect me. I am also very angry. But I don't know how else to tell you." Clearly, it's a desire to communicate, usually after all else has failed.

After as dramatic an act as an attempted suicide, important changes have to be made. Problems and the method of solving them have to be remedied. Doreen's hospital experience has contributed nothing to improving her situation; if anything, it has only made her resolve to suicide properly the next time. Nor has her attempt opened up the lines of communication with her parents: They respond in typical fashion by denying the whole incident—again they don't take her seriously. We know that she is too headstrong to change her ways, so she has two alternatives: She can remain in a bad situation that she has already demonstrated she cannot cope with or she can leave. Because she is strong and determined to survive, she chooses to leave. It's a difficult move for a seventeen-year-old girl to make, certainly more difficult than swallowing a bottle of pills. But Doreen has opted for survival.

Bill's story has much in common with Doreen's. For him, too, suicide is easy. He not only attempts it twice, but his lifestyle is suicidal – Bill is an alcoholic. He, too, doesn't have the respect and recognition from his parents (particularly his father) that he craves so badly. Like Doreen, he doesn't know how to cope effectively when the going gets rough. But the big difference between them is that survival doesn't come easy for Bill.

He begins drinking at an early age because he has discovered early, through the example of his parents, that alcohol is a quick and easy way to feel good about himself. That's a need all of us have; but for Bill, despite all his material advantages, it's a feeling that can only come from a bottle. As he grows older, he finds it more and more difficult to accept the fact that life is not going to play by his rules. He crashes through life, damaging himself and all those in contact with him, but he does not accept any responsibility for himself or his actions. Even his alcoholism is an aspect of his unwillingness to accept responsibility. Karl Menninger, a close follower of Freud, wrote a book called *Man Against Himself*. In it he describes drug addicts and alcoholics as "chronic suicides," who choose to destroy themselves slowly, all the while justifying their actions by claiming that they are only making life more bearable for themselves. They do these self-destructive things because they want to die, but can't accept the responsibility for their own suicide.[5]

Bill knows that he doesn't really like who he is. When Patty wants to delay marrying until he can prove that he can stay dry, he's so afraid of failing the test she has set for him that he immediately starts drinking. He sees himself as a failure, behaves accordingly, and lives up to his own expectations.

When Patty rejects him, he tries to win her back by deliberately trying to make her feel sorry for him. Bill figures it's the only card he has left. With dignity gone, he'll try pity. It's his old childhood trick again. Like Doreen, he plays for very high stakes; if Patty had been delayed in traffic or simply changed her mind about coming, Bill might easily have died.

In his second suicide attempt, Bill has similar manipulative motives, but this time he takes fewer chances. He phones his girlfriend immediately upon taking his drug overdose. The expectation to be saved is common among people who attempt suicide, especially when they don't really intend to die. Sometimes their calculations can go awry. In his enlightening book on suicide, *The Savage God*, A. Alvarez discusses the poet Sylvia Plath's death. All the signs indicated that she really didn't want to die. She turned on the gas and put her head in the oven, knowing that her babysitter was expected soon and would call the doctor, whose number she had conveniently left. But when the babysitter arrived the building was locked. By the time she was able to enter the apartment so much time had elapsed that Sylvia Plath was dead.[6]

As theatrical as the attempted suicides of Doreen and Bill might seem, we should not for a moment ignore the pain, the anger, and the depression that caused them. Neither *wanted* to die; they chose suicide because they didn't know what else to do. Part of their maturing and recovery will involve finding different and better coping mechanisms.

Bill is determined to give survival a good hard try, but if he doesn't make it he knows that an easy suicide awaits him. Suicide, says Alvarez, is like divorce – a confession of failure. "Those who survive suicide, like those who make a new marriage, survive into a changed life with different standards and motives and satisfactions."[7] Both Doreen and Bill will be successful as survivors only if they are capable of change, so that suicide – though easy – becomes an unthinkable solution to the problems of living.

Although Bill and Doreen did not come from grossly disturbed families, a large part of their problems stemmed from the fact that they had certain expectations of their families that could never be met. They derived these expectations directly from social values. We all grow up with the notion that the family is the one social unit that will truly protect and nurture us. Others, such as government or school, may ignore our needs; but we will always have the warmth and support of the family. So we are terribly hurt and disappointed when we find our family lacking in these qualities. In the next chapter we shall see what happens when families are not only unsupportive, but actually cruelly and ruthlessly destructive.

2

WHERE HAVE ALL THE PARENTS GONE?

The wounds of the past will not heal over... The life of the suicide is, to an extraordinary degree, unforgiving. Nothing he achieves by his own efforts, or luck bestows, reconciles him to his injurious past.... A suicide of this kind is born, not made.
A. Alvarez, The Savage God

Greta

I can never remember feeling good about myself. From the time I was a little kid I always felt nobody liked me – not my parents, my brothers, my sister, nobody. I never had any friends, someone I could tell everything to. I tried to make friends, but nobody seemed to care for me. They'd always go back with their other friends and leave me.

I also had a lot of problems with my appearance. Until grade nine I was a head taller than everybody else. The kids always called me names like Stretch and Daddy Long-Legs. I felt the other kids were always laughing at me.

Things weren't much better at home. The only way I could

deal with my problems when I was a little kid – and even now – was to cry a lot. My mother wasn't very sympathetic. The crying bothered her; it got on her nerves.

Nobody in the family ever made an effort to understand me or even to talk to me. My family isn't exactly what you'd call warm. There's never any expressions of love or any feeling. It's a bunch of people living together under the same roof. That's about the size of it because none of us really like each other. I'm eighteen and I can't remember my mother or father ever hugging or kissing us.

Things started getting really bad in high school. I changed schools. In the old school even though I didn't have any friends I still had kids to hang around with; in the new school I had no one. At that age everybody's in groups. I felt out of it. I tried, but I couldn't get along with the others. I didn't like them; they were mostly into parties and drinking. I wasn't into that sort of thing and I felt really strange. I thought something was wrong with me. They thought I was weird. I tried to find kids with my interests and I did try to hang around in this other group. But I didn't have self-confidence and I felt like I was forcing myself on them and they didn't really want me.

High school was pretty much a waste. I felt totally useless. I was bored and depressed and always putting myself down. I figured I've got to stop being the way I am and try to change so that I'll find somebody who would like me. I knew I couldn't let anyone see what I was really like. So I went on a wilderness course and I met one girl that I really liked, Randy. We continued the friendship at home.

The whole thing was very painful. She was very dominant and I'm a follower, so I let her lead me. She was really good with the putdowns. Cutting up was her specialty. It really hurt sometimes. I couldn't tell her about it because I couldn't talk to her. I can't talk to anyone. That's part of my problem.

I hated being touched. Randy came from a family where physical contact doesn't bother anybody. It was nothing to her to give me a punch in the shoulder or to give me a bump that would send me flying across the room. It drove me crazy, but I put up with it.

Then there was this guy I got to like. We all hung around together in a group, Randy included. I never let on how I felt about him because I was too shy. I was just waiting for him to notice me. One day Randy asked me if I wanted to know how he felt about me. I said sure, kind of breathlessly. Then she said, "Rob said that even if you were the last girl on earth he wouldn't go out with you." I was mad as hell at him. I was mad at making a fool of myself. Everyone knew that I liked him. I'm sure Randy didn't lie to me; that's probably how Rob really felt about me. We all still hung around together, but I felt I was being pushed out.

A while later Randy called and said there had to be changes in our friendship. She said, "You're going to have to change." She said I was extremely phoney. I guess I was so ill at ease I came off phoney. I got so tied up in knots that I couldn't act myself. She said I was possessive and that we should cool it for a while. I thought the friendship was over. I started doing a lot of crying.

By this time I'd gotten a job working as a cashier in a supermarket. It was dull and boring. I was getting more and more depressed. I quit the job in October. I wasn't making any motions about getting another job; I just couldn't. My mother was really worried about me. She asked me if I wanted to see a doctor. She thought we'd talk about why I wasn't getting another job. I really wanted to talk about why I was so depressed and everything. Nothing came out of it. The doctor just told me I'd outgrow it; I didn't believe him.

Then came the clincher. I'd been out shopping with my mother and we had a fight. She told me that I was always so much trouble and to get out of her sight and wait for her in the car. I just sat in the car and cried. I really wanted to be my mom's favourite, and all of a sudden it hit me like a sledge hammer. She really hated me and didn't give a damn about me. I was her worst kid. It really hurt.

I started thinking about how my folks brought us up. I blame them a little. For one thing my dad really wasn't in the picture. He didn't bring us up. My mom did. He was just the guy in the background. He was more like a visiting uncle. He never supported us emotionally. He never even talked to us. I really don't like him because he rejected me. My mom says he's like me. He has no self-confidence, so he figured if he didn't come in contact with us it wouldn't rub off on us. Well it backfired, didn't it?

Now I think a lot about suicide. I don't see things changing. I just can't stand it. I think of taking sleeping pills. The thought of slitting my wrists makes me cringe. I fantasize about my mother finding me and wishing she had treated me better. The only drawback is I wouldn't be around to see the results. I tried to tell Randy how I felt, but I can't say things in words. I started to cry and hung up and she was mad. She hated hearing me cry. I tried to tell her about wanting to kill myself, but she had no sympathy. Nothing. I felt she didn't give a damn and I wanted someone to show they did care. And I think I'm going nuts. There has to be something wrong with me if I'm thinking of killing myself.

But I don't see any way out except suicide. My parents couldn't care less if I'm dead or alive. I have no friends, no prospects for the future, and I'm scared of the future. I don't want to get married and have kids. It's a big responsibility and I don't feel confident enough. Mom doesn't seem to enjoy it. I hate the whole world. I'm just a born loser. Wouldn't you think of suicide if you were in my place?

Greta's psychologist

When I first met Greta I saw her as an anxious, depressed teenager. She was able to talk about her depression, but she couldn't go into the reasons for it. She felt she was a misfit at home. She had some general idea about the causes. She had suicidal thoughts that I found frightening, because there was something very desperate about her that made me feel it wasn't just idle talk. I just had the feeling that she would do it because there were no other alternatives available. Greta said that she had always felt that she wasn't cut out for life; there wasn't really that much doing in life that made her happy or wanted, or that gave her a good feeling about what she was doing. She seemed to me to be a very bright girl who had not utilized her potential. I could see her in university, for example: that could have happened very easily for her. But her family didn't direct her that way; they just didn't care.

Greta's background was very middle class. The predominant feature was that basically the marital situation was very bad – the parents just hated each other and admitted it. Mother was a very bright, very put-together person. Dad was passive. Mother was able to say that they were completely different and that she had no respect for him. She felt his involvement with her and the children was non-existent. She referred to him as a visiting uncle. But despite all that hostility the marriage persisted – not only for the sake of the children, but they just seemed unwilling to dissolve it. Father was too passive to take any action and Mother contented herself with the fact that he had a good management job.

I think Mother may have resented Greta right from the start because she was an unplanned pregnancy. She also felt that Greta was a child you couldn't get close to or cuddle because of her size. That's stunning when you think about it. In a retrospective fashion, Mother felt that Greta demonstrated signs of emotional difficulty early on. Once when her mother was entertaining other kids at a birthday party, Greta just flew out of the room and slammed the door in a rage. She was about five at the time. Generally she found Greta snarky, unlikable and unlovable, somewhat temperamental, and a pain to have. All this seems to me to suggest that Greta was different from the other kids in her family in that she demanded more than she got. When her mother didn't meet these demands through inability, it triggered off the enormous problems that Greta has today.

Greta got thinly disguised messages from her mother about her position in the family, which is, "Frankly, my dear, you're a pain in the ass." So what can a kid do? They have to grope with those terrible feelings of inadequacy. It's sad that parents find it hard to compliment kids and bolster their self-esteem, but they are just so tied up in their own problems. *The parents who are supportive usually produce kids who are more intact emotionally and socially.*

To be fair, I don't think all the blame should go to Mother. Father gets his share, too. In many ways he was more of a problem. He was very cold and distant. One of the ways a girl grows to feel that she is a woman is by the way her dad pays attention to her. Because Greta wasn't getting that from her father, what feelings was she getting about growing into womanhood? A girl who wonders about her womanhood wants to know what Dad thinks and maybe rates herself on that. And if her dad is giving her cold messages, then she's going to start feeling guilty, unfeminine, and maybe a lot of other things, too. What was reinforcing Greta's feelings of worthlessness was a father saying, "I'm not even noticing you." That's pretty hard for a kid to accept.

Greta hates her father. Maybe it's good that she does, because before she realized that she had a right to hate him she was internalizing that anger towards herself, and that's one of the big things that was making her so damned depressed. Depression is anger turned inwards. One of the goals in therapy is to make her see that it's okay not to like Dad. Sometimes a parent isn't always together either.

When you look at teenagers, one of the most important things to look at is their relations with peers. Do they have any good friends? You find that kids who don't relate well are the ones who usually have trouble, then and in later life. Greta never seemingly had good peer relationships. Her so-called best friend on whom she was extremely reliant really abused her and kept adding to the negative image she had of herself. She became very jealous when this girl would do something with another girl. Greta just couldn't let go because she was so unsure of herself.

I can never tell Mother anything that goes on in therapy because that's one of our ethics, so she's never been told explicitly that Greta has strong suicidal thoughts; but she knows it anyway. She treats it in a very simplistic way. She thinks that everybody has these thoughts, and she plays them down. She doesn't ever really worry about it. If Greta ever makes an attempt, Mother will be desperately upset and guilty.

It's difficult to say whether or not Greta will make it. She's got a lot of strikes against her. Nothing is going to help until she starts getting out and doing things, but how can a person who's feeling so low get out and do things? I don't know what will happen. You must realize that a lot of adolescents work things out for themselves if they have the resources, but does Greta have the resources? She's bright. She's got a fair degree of insight. I think she's starting to realize that just because Mom and Dad maybe weren't the most loving, caring parents didn't necessarily mean that she wasn't lovable. As long as that issue is reinforced with her, I think she has a chance to succeed.

Lenore

The most significant factor in my background is that between the ages of thirteen and fourteen I was regularly assaulted by my father. When it came to the court's attention, even though there was documented proof, nobody believed me. Everybody made it quite clear that they could not accept that as the way it happened. Even the psychiatrists told me about the naughty things girls say about their daddies when they're mad at them, and from that point on I felt different, abnormal, and that there was something wrong with my brain.

My father wasn't drunk or anything; he was just strange. He tried to force us to like him, but we couldn't. If we weren't nice to him he'd sexually assault not only me, but my brother and sister. My mother just stood by and watched. She was a silent bystander. She couldn't believe it even though he beat her up, too. One day my mother left the house to go to work. He told me to stay home so he could touch me and everything. I wouldn't listen and left the house. When I got home he beat me until I was totally black and blue. My mother watched the whole thing and didn't even try to stop him. All she said was, "Wait till you get married. Then you'll understand."

To make matters worse I had no one to talk to. Everyone at school knew about my father. It was in the papers. I went into my shell and separated myself from other people. Right through high school I didn't have anything to do with anybody else, and it didn't bother me. I preferred it that way. I was tired of being put down and humiliated by people accepting me and then turning their backs on me when they found out all about my background.

I first knew I was cracking up when I was fourteen. I bit my hand as hard as I could and I drew blood. I called my mom and said, "Look! I need help." And she said, "There's a good movie on downstairs and we have company." At the time I really felt like a fool. But now, looking at it from a different perspective, I could boot her ass for her reaction.

It wasn't long after that I made my first suicide attempt. I remember I was going with my mother and sister to a roadside stand to buy some corn. I had taken two bottles of sleeping pills before we left and I told my mother what I had done a few minutes after we got into the car. She said, "I hope you're happy. Now we can't go to get corn. We'll have to go to the hospital to have your stomach pumped." I said, "Well just forget it then." And she forgot it. I went home and slept it off. I guess the pills weren't too powerful.

The next time I tried it I was going out with a guy. He told me he never wanted to see me again. Nothing else in my life was really worth living for. I think that's really common when you're an adolescent. You don't have the alternatives you have as an adult. Nowadays I think if that happened to me I wouldn't think of killing myself. I'd leave the city, start a new life. When you're an adolescent in high school with your parents controlling you, you don't have the alternatives. Suicide is about the only one. Either continue the way you're going or kill yourself. You can't cope with problems and accept disappointment because past a certain point you don't have the means to cope.

Altogether I made ten suicide attempts. I felt that the only time I would be taken seriously was if I were dead. Even in the hospital no one took me seriously. Last time I was in, the nurse said something like, "We hope you'll think twice before you do this again." Never a matter of them bringing in a psychiatrist. Just "Oh Christ, you again!" Get it out of me and go home. They don't want to see you again. I'm surprised that I kept going through it.

A friend asked me why I used only sleeping pills. I didn't have the courage to do it the painful ways. I also knew if I didn't succeed those ways I'd be in bigger trouble, because I'd have the physical scars. Sleeping pills are convenient; it's not that I thought chances of succeeding with them were less. And sleeping pills are really easy to come by. Many doctors in this city are more than happy to give young people any kind of pill they want. One doctor in particular knew I was suicidal. Had my counsellor not phoned him up and told him not to give me another pill I could still go in there and get anything I wanted. It was common knowledge around the city, but this doctor never lost his licence. Kids in school get to know which doctors will give pills.

Obviously, despite all my attempts at suicide and the availability of pills, I'm still around. I can't tell you why I did it — every case is different. Sometimes I did it for attention, but mostly, I think, for relief. I was looking for a way out; for peace. A couple of times I was saved because I called the local distress centre. It was important to hear their love and warmth on the phone. They let you know they want you to live. You could always say that my attempts weren't very serious if I called the centre. But you see, sleeping pills have a relaxing effect and you aren't too aware of what you're doing. I'm sure there were times when, if I hadn't had a phone available, I wouldn't have even thought of calling them. It was something to do while it felt so good, and they were always so kind and responsive.

I stopped attempting suicide when I finally got into the type of relationship that made me feel worthwhile. Once accepted by one person I was able to develop other relationships. Just having someone who loves me, knows my past, accepts it, and makes me feel I'm okay enabled me to go out and create other relationships for myself.

If my fiancé broke up with me or any other really stressful thing happened to me I don't think I'd try suicide again. Now I'm an adult I can change things for myself. I don't have to face kids at school tomorrow. I can move away, start over. I've redirected the anger from myself towards the people who make me angry. I no longer blame other people's ignorance on myself, and that's what therapy taught me. That I'm okay. I'm not a freak, I'm not really suicidal. And I can say that despite the fact that I know that I'm still an obstacle in my parents' life. My mother still gives me a lot of negative feedback, and so do my brother and sister.

I've also learned that anger can be a positive thing. If I wasn't able to go up to my room and scream, I'd just go off the deep end like I used to. I let it out as soon as it comes. To clear my conscience completely when I'm older I'm going to tell my parents how I feel about them. Only by clearing the air completely can I have a half-decent relationship with them. They know they're failures. They are children themselves.

I'm not saying that everything is perfect now. I don't have a normal sex life; I'm afraid of it. And I don't want to bring children into this world, especially with the kind of grandfather they'd have. And my whole family is so weird. My sister and brother always denied my dad's sexual assaults. Within the last year my sister finally told me it happened to her, too. My brother almost killed himself. He's escaped the city now. My grandmother and grandfather on the paternal side killed themselves. There is a history of mental illness. Experts have different theories about whether it's inherited. Obviously something in my dad's past made him go a bit funny and I'm afraid it might happen to me.

I could never have come this far myself. I owe a great deal to my counsellor. He made me develop emotionally. I wasn't a person before; I was something that people could abuse any way they wanted. He made me say to hell with the rest of them. It was easy for me to establish a relationship with him because he worked at the distress centre, so it was via the phone at first. I would have found it very hard to start face to face, especially since other professionals had put me down and made me feel bad. Half the battle is getting it all out, and it's been my experience that professionals are going to judge me. An anonymous person is best.

Most young people know someone who has tried suicide. Sharing our experiences could be constructive if we could accept one another. At a fraternity party we were discussing suicide and everyone there admitted having had serious suicidal thoughts. They are glad they didn't succeed. Things get so much better. The years between thirteen and nineteen years are a freaky time for everyone even though my circumstances were a lot more unusual. If you can just ride it out, it really does get better.

The biggest advantage is to feel confident and loved at home. If that happens then nothing else can really affect you too badly. Parents, make your kids feel valuable. Verbalize your positive feelings towards them.

Lenore's counsellor

Lenore has learned new coping mechanisms. In her early attempts, especially, she was seeking peace. She would have been happy to sleep for two years. That's a very difficult kind of suicidal to work with. Others can be convinced that they don't really want to die, or be frightened by the risk if there is not an afterlife; but Lenore just wanted peace, and believed she could get it through death. Hard argument to refute. Eventually her motivation changed. Her gestures became a cry for help. That was easier to deal with because she didn't have to be convinced of a reason to live.

She was constantly being put down by her family. Remember that Lenore was the one who went to the police about her father.

He went to jail because of it and, despite the fact that her brother and sister were also sexually abused by him, she was blamed and made to feel guilty. She also couldn't relate positively to her brother, who reminded her a lot of her father. Her sister was a real case. She's a psychiatric nurse, so she really understood how to hurt Lenore and how to say things to impede her psychological progress. She would tell her that she's really crazy and would end up in a mental hospital. Of course she didn't want Lenore to get better because that would change the family dynamics. She would no longer be the family scapegoat.

And Lenore felt that she had to love *all these people. In a word, they just didn't give a damn about her. They'd sit around watching television while she announced that she was going to her room to kill herself. Nobody ever talked to her about it. She was just another piece of garbage in the house causing trouble, and if she died, that was all right.*

Yet on the phone her mother gave the impression of being a very caring and devoted parent. But that had to be just for show; the facts of Lenore's life negate any positive image her mother may have tried to portray. I tried on many occasions to meet with the parents to discuss Lenore, but every time I tried her mother turned it down.

As if that whole scene with her family wasn't enough, the first psychiatrist she saw really placed a load of guilt on her. He told her that little girls often entice sexual responses from their fathers, and he insinuated that she was to blame. By the time she called us she was really down and wanted someone to talk to about it. I happened to be on duty the first time she called, so I talked to her. Whenever she'd call back she'd ask for me. We developed a good relationship over the phone, but it took seven months till she consented to see me. And I think she did only because I happened to say something that really appealed to her. During one of our conversations I conjured up a very romantic analogy for her of an adolescent fighting her way through the mud. You come through the murk and eventually start to see life. Break the surface and you have the whole universe. This is where she was at. This image gave her hope. She also felt very safe in dealing with me because I'm homosexual.

Lenore had and still does have a lot of problems that came about directly as a result of her family experience. Not surprisingly, she has a constant fear of males – sexual fears. Yet she needs a lot of safety and cuddling. Attempts to get these would invariably lead to sexual relationships that were not her goal. If she got a man to give her the attention she wanted she would then smother him, so that the relationship became very one-sided. Invariably she would choose rich, handsome, influential men because she's status oriented and this gave her confidence. When they rejected her, that would precipitate a suicide attempt. She'd see herself as worthless and having nothing else to live for.

Despite the fact that she gives the impression of being a very sexually enticing person, she can't face the consequences. A good sexual relationship is very difficult for her to achieve. She's never chosen to work sexual problems through. She prefers to keep them buried, though she's aware of the games she plays in trading off sexual favours for physical closeness.

And, of course, she still has problems about her family, mainly because her feelings about them are so confused. Lenore hates her mother who blames her and allows her to be sexually abused by her husband, yet she also feels gratitude towards her mother for some of the material luxuries she's provided. As far as her father is concerned, she feels both pity and contempt for him. She can't direct her anger towards him and she still feels guilty because he's sick and was in prison. I often think she'd do best by just writing her parents off, but she can't bring herself to do it. She still wants them to love her.

Lenore has come a long way. She has more inner strength, and more coping ability knowing that she can change her situation. Now at university she's become very active and is somewhat of a public figure on campus, and she's not that bothered by others' criticisms of her. That's remarkable when you consider all the crap she was fed as a child, so that she had no positive self-image with which to relate to others. But something still bothers me. I don't think she has peace even now. I think she deliberately keeps herself too busy for introspection.

Mark

I was nine years old when I first started drinking, but I didn't get into it seriously till I was twelve. I'm seventeen now. All my troubles started off with my drinking. Things just weren't working out for me, and I'd just take it out on myself with booze. After drinking for a couple of weeks I'd get sick; sometimes I'd end up in the hospital.

I started drinking because both my parents were alcoholics. My mother died when I was six. My father turned into a real alcoholic then. You'd think that seeing such a bad example, I would want to stay away from it; and when I was ten I tried. When I got to be eleven I started back into it, nipping beer off my father and my uncle. Then, when I was twelve, I started getting into trouble. I started fighting and stealing things to drink. That just got me into deeper trouble and it kept on building up.

When I look back I see that I started drinking more or less because I was unhappy, and it was a way to make me feel better. I knew from watching older people that if you were really down, booze could make you feel better. Just before my father passed away he said he didn't want me to drink. I thought about it for a while, then I said that's a bunch of garbage. He went out drinking, why can't I? I just kept repeating to myself, "I'm really alone now," and it got drilled into my skull that I was gonna become a loner. Nobody could tell me what to do. I did my own thing and just kept on going.

When I was about fifteen I made an attempt at suicide by jumping out of a window. I landed in the hospital for that. I remember everything except right after jumping out the window. I split my head open and got twelve stitches across my forehead. I was in the hospital for three weeks, in the psychiatric ward. I really freaked out there. I was kind of mad that I failed. I guess I wanted to be dead with my parents. I thought I'd be happier that way. As an Indian, my view of death or life after death may be different from yours. I really believe that when you die you still live. You come back in a different form. So in suicide I was just ending this life, not all life, so I wasn't afraid to do it.

It wasn't really planned. The night before I was drinking and talking to a friend, and I said I should kill myself because I want to be with my parents. He said that was no way to go about it. So I started to get mad at him and I left. I kept on drinking and I went back to his place that night. I passed out there and started drinking again the next morning. I passed out and got up again and drank some more. That's when I jumped out of the window. It was about nine o'clock I guess. I don't remember getting to the hospital or anything. It's kind of hard to describe what happened in the psychiatric ward. After a couple of days I came back to my mind and wondered why I was there. I was mad because I had failed.

For the next three years I was in and out of a boys' home. I was getting fed up with that place and I figured I could handle the pressure on the outside, but I couldn't. I was only fooling myself. Every time I'd be out I'd get into trouble and enjoy it.

Just when I turned sixteen I got into a fight. My arm got slashed and I took sixteen stitches for that. That really bothered me, and I went after the person. I was going to kill him, and then kill myself. I found the guy but I didn't kill him. I just knocked out a couple of his teeth and broke a couple of his ribs. I thought that was lots of fun, so I started getting into more trouble.

I started rolling people for drinking money. I hardly ever bought things for myself. I just drank, drank, drank. That got pretty sickening afterwards. I turned to dope. My father and grandfather had told me lots of things like that I'd either die or end up in a psychiatric ward, but I didn't pay any attention to that. I did a lot of grass, and I started on acid for a while. Then I got picked up again. That's where it stopped me. I just didn't want to do it anymore.

I don't know why, but all of a sudden I really wanted to go straight. Life was too miserable for me the other way. The drinking and the fighting were getting to me. I guess losing my parents was like the end of the world. I just didn't want to go on. I didn't know how.

Slowly but surely I'm starting to get everything together now. I realize that I should try to make something of myself while I still can.

There's some people that have the power to do that, but they just don't want to. They're afraid of failing. Now I'm not afraid of failing. You just keep on trying and build yourself up. Once you do that you start getting what you need. You don't go around asking people for things you want. You can't depend on people all of the time to support you or give you everything. It's gotta come from you. Nowadays there's a lot of young people that haven't even gone to school. When I realized that I was going to straighten out, I said to myself that I should try to help these people out. I don't like seeing young kids getting into trouble. When I was in trouble there was nobody around to help me.

I'm trying to go straight now, cut out the drinking and the dope, and find a girl that's right for me. That's important to me. And get a job and settle down. Just sit back and take life easy. There's no other way. I want independence, peace of mind, and self-respect. I'd like for people to look up to me as a person who's trying to help somebody else. Not like a drunk or a fighter. I've got plans to go back to school.

When I was drinking I was angry and I didn't like myself. Now I'm not angry any more and I like myself a lot better. I still miss my parents, and sure, some day I'll join them; but not before I've done something with my life first.

In a recent Gallup poll comparing the success of family life now as compared with that of a generation ago, three-quarters of those asked thought it less successful now. Ten years ago when the same question was asked more people thought there had been an enrichment in family life than those who saw a deterioration.[1]

This information is probably not startling in its newness, but the implications that it contains are shattering, particularly for children. Not only does the family represent the most important social unit in our society, but it is the one in which children are supposed to be nurtured, loved, and taught so that they can grow into responsible adults. Surely no one would argue with the conclusion that so many more teenagers today are attempting and committing suicide because they don't get enough from their families to sustain them in life.

Social scientists agree that the motives for suicide in young people cannot be fully understood without carefully considering their family situations. A significant number of young people who attempt suicide come from broken or disorganized homes, where at least one parent is absent and quarrelling is frequent. Alcoholism or poverty may be a factor, and there may often be cruelty or rejection.[2] These factors are so detrimental because they don't lend themselves to creating an environment of love and support.

Evidence of the disintegrating family is all around us. More than one out of three marriages end in divorce, and usually there are children involved. It's not uncommon for children to feel responsible for their parents' divorce, and therefore guilty; at the same time they feel rejected by the parent who leaves without them. Mother, the parent in our society who traditionally does most of the nurturing of children, is now fulfilling a bread-winning role as well. Because of the climbing divorce rate, economic necessity, and the emotional need of many women for stimulation other than that from children, many mothers do work outside the home, and the care their children get while they are away may not always be adequate. Because of the widespread absence of good daycare facilities, low-income families are particularly affected, as they are the ones who can't afford the costly alternative of private care.

The increased mobility that characterizes our lifestyle means that young people might be deprived of a sense of stability if their families move around a lot. A major move is particularly difficult to cope with during adolescence, when belonging to a group is extremely important, for it can be very difficult to break into a new group. The loneliness and isolation that a young person feels in such a situation can be incapacitating.

Our mobility has also considerably reduced the extended family. With grandparents often hundreds or even thousands of miles away, many teenagers are strangers to the continuity and security of the family as it used to be. With their extended family scattered and their nuclear family possibly deteriorating, they have little sense of belonging, of tradition, and of the role they will play in society.

All this is compounded by the phenomenon of doing your own thing, which we discussed earlier. Adolescence is normally a time when children separate from their parents in order to establish themselves as individuals. Today that separation is often made final and irrevocable because caring involves responsibility, and it's often more convenient not to have that responsibility – for parents as well as for children. This is seen most clearly in our attitude towards the elderly. If many adults ignore their parents, they set an example for their own children to follow in treating their parents. Neglect becomes a tradition.

In any suicide attempt of any young person it's frequently easy to blame the parents, but too often the parents find themselves in situations where they have no love to give. If the family is deteriorating, parents are going to feel it, too.

A woman whose husband has left her, and who is forced to support her children and herself, will have a tough time conveying to her children that she really does care about them when she works all day and comes home exhausted. All she may want is some supper, a hot bath, and a good night's sleep. The added responsibility of children may be more than she can handle. Although she loves them, that feeling may never come through. She is so concerned about meeting their physical needs that she neglects their emotional ones.

A parent who is an alcoholic may abuse his child, not wilfully, but because he himself copes so badly with life, as manifested in his drinking, that any additional pressure is unbearable. Or parents who don't get along, but who stay together "for the sake of the children," genuinely believing that they are acting in the children's best interests, are often so consumed with bitterness and frustration that whatever love they may be capable of expressing gets lost. The examples are endless. The point is that parents can be poor parents because circumstances make it impossible for them to be anything else. The message that comes across is, "Get lost, kid. I've got problems of my own." Tragically, their children often take them literally.

Then there are parents who are extremely concerned with self-fulfilment. That goal is often incompatible with raising children. It's an ideological bind that many parents get caught in. Marriages are supposed to produce children, but what do you do with the children once you have them if you're trying to discover yourself? Bill's family life was an example of that. His parents were so involved in their own pursuits that they just didn't have the time or the interest to give him any attention or discipline. Everything that they did – or didn't do – conveyed the message, "You're on your own, kid. We can't be bothered." It doesn't automatically follow that all parents who seek to fulfil themselves will automatically ignore their children; but there is a fine line between self-fulfilment and selfishness.

To illustrate parental indifference to children a lawyer who specializes in family law and who has handled many divorce and custody cases said, "It used to be that when a couple divorced the mother would automatically get the kids. A few years ago fathers started fighting for custody. Now, it seems that nobody wants them."

Dr. Herbert Hendin, in his book *The Age of Sensation*, argues that the increase in adolescent suicide is due to the fact that children are programmed by their parents to kill themselves. In an age that emphasizes maximum personal expression and self-gratification, many parents don't want their children to be conspicuous and to bother them. They don't want to sacrifice for their children. They resent having to do things that don't provide instant gratification, and the results of child-rearing are far from instant. The children get the message. They "grow up dead" and are drawn to suicide "because deadness has been their only security for a lifetime."[3]

A psychologist who works in the emergency room of a major hospital tells a story that sadly corroborates Hendin's theory.

"There was one family I saw where the boy and girl were really mixed up. The mother said to them in my presence, 'If you do that again I'll call Children's Aid to take you away.' She really wanted to get rid of them. She was obviously a poor mother. She was a neurotic, self-centred, middle-class person who never should have been a mother. She had a lot of ideas about appropriate behaviour, which was having a home, a boy and a girl, which was just what she had; but she never wanted the kids. She resented the demands they made on her time, and the fact that they weren't neat and orderly. She just resented their existence. Something I find interesting is that as they grew into teenagers they developed an incestuous sexual relationship, and they were both suicidal. But the only love they had was each other, literally, so they held on pretty hard.

"What really brought them here was that the girl was in emergency because of an overdose. When the mother got here she said, 'Thank God. You can take them off my hands. They're beyond me.' She knew about the sexual relationship and hadn't talked about it. She was just disgusted with it. She hadn't done anything about it, but her reaction was if she ever heard of this happening again she would call Children's Aid.

"She was on her second husband who was younger than her and she was working very hard at keeping him. She really focused on this man – not the kids' father – as though that was all she cared about. There was just no room for children."

The terrible irony of family breakdown seems to be that the more a child is rejected by his parents, the more he tries and needs to love them. Over and over again young people who recounted their experiences with suicide indicated that even though the trouble had been because of their parents, they still sought to love them and to be reconciled with them. Sadly, some even blamed themselves for their troubled family situation. In one girl's family both parents drank so heavily that she and her brothers were taken from them and placed in foster homes, where she had spent most of her life. She's been an alcoholic, delinquent, and suicidal. When asked if she hated her family, she said, "Oh, no. My family really cares about me. I'm not bitter. I love them too much. I hate to see them drink and see what happens to them. Sometimes I think they're drinking because of me. Especially my mom."

There is something pathetic and yet noble about the human spirit that will not only survive great violations, but will be prepared to give love even where it cannot be found.

From reading Greta's story, we're likely to come away with the impression that part of her problem is that she's not very good looking. Actually, she is stunning. Tall, statuesque, with curly blond hair and the complexion of a Botticelli angel, it's difficult to imagine that this girl views herself as a loser who has problems with her appearance. But then, how is she supposed to know how beautiful she is when no one has told her? To the contrary, she has been teased by her "friends," shunned by her mother, and ignored by her father.

We are angry at the way she has been treated by her family because they seem so uncaring and so unjust. Yet we see that there can be no other way; her family just can't meet her needs. Her parents are emotionally impoverished people who are not equipped to deal with a bright, shy, sensitive daughter who demands more than the other children because she needs more. Because their own resources are so limited they resent her; she's an added stress they can't handle. In Hendin's terms her family would feel more comfortable with her if she were "lifeless" and caused no trouble. But she is still not "emotionally extinct." To please her parents she will have to learn to have no feelings and to make no demands. To please herself, she will have to break away – if she can.

Greta's situation is a terribly exaggerated version of Doreen's, but unlike Mark, Lenore, and Doreen, she's not a fighter. She doesn't have that determination and strength to go out and do something about herself. We wonder, somewhat bitterly, if her family hasn't already done her in.

Mark is an inspiration. His recovery is nothing short of

miraculous. Without the benefit of guidance, encouragement, or support from his parents, indeed without any positive examples from them, Mark decides to take hold of his life, reverse its suicidal direction, and take responsibility for his actions.

Like Bill, he learns at an early age from his parents about the magical escape powers of alcohol, and like Bill, he uses them to create a suicidal lifestyle because he has a lot to escape from. Although as an Indian he may believe in life after death, there is nothing particularly Indian about his desire to rejoin his parents through death. It's well known that a child who loses a parent through death will sometimes attempt suicide in an effort to rejoin him.[4] But Mark's suicide attempt is not made solely so that he can be with his parents once again; for him, as for so many others, suicide is the way out of a painful existence.

His delinquent behaviour is closely related to his suicidal desires; in fact, suicide and delinquency are opposite sides of the same coin. Simply put, as Freud first saw it, suicide is hostility turned against the self, while delinquency is hostility turned outward against society.[5] It is indicative of all the same things as suicide: loneliness, despair, and an inability to cope. In some ways delinquency is healthier, simply because the aggression is outwardly directed, and it is at the very least an indication of the position the young person has taken: he is determined to fight. In her sympathetic portrayal of delinquent girls, Gisela Konopka writes:

> As long as a girl fights through her loneliness she is still healthy. She may become a nuisance to society and she will suffer, but there is a healthy spark which allows for change. The one who gives in to the loneliness, who ceases to fight, is the seriously disturbed one. Those are the girls who make suicide attempts or take drugs or who start the flight into mental illness.[6]

Why Mark renounces his old ways of suicide and delinquency is clear: he wants to count for something in this world. But how he is able to do it is a mystery. Somewhere in his stormy life he must have learned pride, and somewhere deep inside him he must have had a reservoir of strength waiting to be tapped. If we knew how it got there we would perhaps be able to explain why some people commit suicide while others struggle and survive.

Lenore impresses us more by what she doesn't say than by what she says. Nowhere does she express feelings of anger against her parents, particularly her father. We not only expect her to, we want her to. But she can't do it. That's the big problem with almost all suicidal people: they can't express anger, so they internalize it where it festers. It's easy for us to want her to be free of her parents, but for her to do that is to acknowledge that love from them will never be forthcoming. Surely the most painful realization any child can come to is the knowledge that his parents never have and never will love him.

What saves Lenore is her great willingness to do battle against the forces that seek to destroy her. Paradoxically, she is herself one of these forces. Because she's never passive about her problems, as Greta is, she seeks help. Fortunately, the distress centre worked for her; it wouldn't be an exaggeration to say that it saved her life. The ready availability of immediate sympathetic contact, the protective anonymity, and the assurance that the listener is not going to be judgemental makes a telephone crisis centre one of the miracle-workers of the twentieth century. As one long-time telephone counsellor put it, "People call the centre because they don't want to die. I reach out and I say, 'I don't want you to die either.' Often that's all a person has to hear to keep him alive a little longer, till he can find better ways of dealing with his problems." But crisis lines don't solve all problems; they can't, after all, respond to people who don't take the first step to contact them, and some suicidal people simply aren't capable of the little initiative it takes to pick up the phone to say, "I need help."

Lenore is also able to find one meaningful relationship with another person, one who accepts her and loves her for what she is. That is perhaps the greatest factor in the prevention of suicide—to know that there is one person who cares and who says, "I value you. You are a worthwhile person." How much better might Bill, Greta or Mark have fared if they had had that?

Finally, Lenore makes it because time is on her side. She reaches the point in her development at which she outlives her adolescence, so that she can say, "I'm not a kid anymore. I can change things now." That attitude implies a willingness to accept responsibility for the direction of one's own life. Lenore wants that responsibility. Bill too has survived beyond adolescence, but he didn't have the strength to make that commitment until much later. Age does not automatically bring with it the capacity for change.

If we are to accept the view of Lenore's counsellor, then we can anticipate that the going will be rough for her because she isn't yet introspective enough. But Lenore is a survivor. She has come through a nightmare and has awakened bruised, but intact. What time will not heal she will probably learn to live with in her own way. Too much introspection can paralyze one's desire to fight for survival.

Lenore urges all parents to make their kids feel worthwhile, and to *tell* them so. It would be very easy to say, "Well of course Greta, Mark, and Lenore were suicidal. No one ever made them feel worthwhile or wanted. They came from grossly disturbed families." But what of the thousands of adolescents attempting suicide who come from supposedly normal families, whose parents sincerely believe that they are following Lenore's advice to the letter? We shall meet them in the next chapter.

3

TESTING, TESTING – SHOW ME THAT YOU LOVE ME

If suicide is a cry for help, then the young, even in their self-destruction, remain optimistic . . . They still believe that something or someone will turn up.
A. Alvarez, The Savage God

Howard

I first attempted suicide when I was fourteen. I was the smartest kid in the school; I came from a good home in a very good neighbourhood. But one day it finally happened. I took fifty of my mother's tranquillizers to school and swallowed them just before a gym class.

The problems began when I started high school. Before that nobody ever put me down for being the smartest kid. But in high school I had to be bussed with all the senior high school kids. And all of a sudden every day on the school bus I kept getting hit and shoved and yelled at by the boys. The girls

58

would sit at the front of the bus and the boys would sit at the back. I'd go to the back of the bus and no one would let me sit with them. They would tell me to go sit with the girls. I wouldn't. I would just stand there and say nothing and let them hit me. I wouldn't ever yell or cry. I would just stand there and let them do whatever they wanted to me. They would leave me a seat and let me sit down and then push me off and let me fall to the ground, open my work, make fun of it and rip it up – things like that.

You see, I had this really sentimental thing. We had this piece of land that had magnolia trees on it and I thought it was so beautiful that I used to call it my fairy land. I told my very best friend about it, and he happened to get mad at me and told everyone else. And I was the smartest kid, so that my fairy-land fantasy meant that I was a fag, a fruit. That was the big laugh at the back of the bus. I was easy to pick on because I wasn't just smart; I was obnoxious. I let everyone know I was smart. And I didn't fight back.

Things started to come down on me really heavily. Until I started high school I was incredibly good at sports. I was into baseball and football and just everything. But in the first two months of high school that whole thing just died out. I couldn't go to gym. I got sick every day. Things like that. I had a really bad reaction to that whole situation. I wouldn't go to school some days; I'd beg my mother to let me stay home. I was too proud to tell my mom and dad what was going on. I couldn't tell them that I was being beaten up and called a fruit. My mother had always told me that I could be anything I wanted to be. My father always said, "You're a Davis. You have to have a sense of pride." They always put this big expectation on me that I had to be good, and I had to be perfect, and everything had to be right with me. I didn't want to tell them that things were that bad, that I couldn't make it in school.

In retrospect I think they would have tried to help me because we're really close now and I know they care. But at the time the main thing going through my head was, "I can't disappoint them. They've given me so much." I couldn't do that to them. So I felt really cut off.

All I was ever told was, "You can do it." That pattern was established very early on. In the early grades there were never many problems for me because I never had any friends. I did nothing but school to please my parents. But then in high school, when I had to start dealing with all these peer people it became an incredibly big problem for me. And I had no background, no tools to deal with it in any way. I hadn't been taught. To tell me that I could do it without being shown how just wasn't good enough. Now I know I can't do it. I need people. But then I assumed that I just had to do it on my own.

I once asked for psychiatric help. My mother's response was, "You can't be sick. You're not sick," and in parentheses I guess what she was saying was, "I don't want to think you're sick. I don't want to think I failed." Their solution was to send me to military school. I interpreted that as, "Here I am finally admitting to you that I have a problem and you want to get rid of me. You want to hide me." Of course I couldn't talk to them about it. I just went into my room and cried.

I know now that I was angry at the time, but I had to repress it. It always made me feel guilty to show it. My mother would say, "Your getting angry makes me upset. I haven't done anything to you." And then she'd start crying. She had this big intellectual thing about anger, that if we could just talk we wouldn't need to get angry. And so I just stopped. I just put it all inside. I decided I had to do it all on my own and wouldn't talk to them about the problems at school.

What finally precipitated the suicide attempt was the kid I had told my fantasy to about the magnolia trees. I finally had the nerve to ask him directly whether he was the one who told them that. I knew he had to be because he was the only one I ever told. And he said, "No. I would never do that to you." I let that lie stand and said, "Well that's really good because I think you're a friend of mine and I really need someone right now." And then I went through the whole thing with him about how I was scared, and how I was getting really upset because I wanted to be one of the guys, and my parents were going to send me away. And the next day when I got on the school bus they all started to come at me with, "Ha, ha. You can never be one of the guys. You should sit up with the girls." That was it. And added to that was the fact that home, my last retreat, was being taken away from me.

The night before I did it I was thinking about death, which always scares me and scared me even more back then. I felt I wanted out. I felt I didn't ask for this. I didn't ask to be born. No one asked me if I wanted to be here. And then my parents didn't want me. So I figured if no one wants me, I don't want myself. I just didn't want to face that situation even one day more.

After they pumped out my stomach and my parents were in the hospital to see me, their big reaction was disgust. "How could you do this to us? What about your little sister? What's wrong with you? Why didn't you tell us? You're doing so well in school." They were really ashamed. And that just set me off on a whole other cycle. Because I should have gotten angry and again it got squelched inside. I cried. That's all I did. I didn't argue with them. I then cut them off and built a very strong defensive shield around me for the rest of my school years.

What I proceeded to do was to build myself up on the model of a Christian martyr. I've always been really religious. No one else in the family is, but I have been. So the Church taught me the meaning of martyrdom and how one person alone who is right can confront the whole world and never have to communicate with them — which was the important part of it. I could be perfect and right, and never have to deal with anyone, and I did. I did very well in school and then finally found a niche that would protect me from all the kids beating me up. And that was to go into radical politics and dope, and confrontations with the teachers. I got expelled. Once I got expelled everything was fine, because I was accepted.

I built this whole shell and convinced myself that I knew the right way in the world. Anyone who wouldn't listen to me or wouldn't take it was the enemy, was evil. That gave me the headspace that very comfortably led me to very radical kinds of things. Then the war in Vietnam started and it gave me the reason for living. From that time on I was fine, until I had a breakdown.

My whole participation in the anti-war movement was, I think, a veiled suicide attempt. I don't like to say it because there were a lot of good reasons to be in it, but mine was self-destruction. My logical motive was altruistic, but the way in which I carried it out was destructive. I was totally belligerent, ramming walls, breaking windows, the whole bit. I was just pushing it to the limit. I was pushing my own head to the limit with all the drugs I was doing, too. One day it finally broke. Right before that happened I was thinking a lot about my suicide, and realized it failed. I guess by that time I felt that I had to have a breakdown.

I realized that things were really wrong, that I wasn't thinking right, that somehow I just wasn't together. I felt that living was not always to fight people, that somehow there had to be some love in it, and the whole love-war double message bothered me. They were always together, especially in rock music. (Music has always been a huge part in my life. The Jefferson Airplane, primarily.) But there were always these messages: "Up against the wall, mother fuckers. We will build a community of love." I got the "Up against the wall" fine, but I never got any of the "Community of love." That's what finally did it. There's something just not right.

I wanted to break myself down and then build myself back up. That was my goal. I wanted to go through the schizophrenic journey because I felt I needed it.

If I hadn't had that breakdown, I'd be dead now – by my own hand. Up until the breakdown I had told everyone that a fortune-teller said I'd be dead by twenty-two. I was too clever to be so obvious as to say "the year you become an adult," so I said twenty-two. I told everyone that was going to happen so I would have to make it happen, because I couldn't have all these people laughing at me. I really saw myself doing that. I knew I was doing it, so I was pretty convinced it would happen. I was a Davis and I was committed. Once you've said it you have to go through with it. You never go back on your word and stay part of the family.

What made me do it in the first place was that I wanted everyone to know how upset I was. I wanted people to know how weak I really was, because my whole belligerent thing was so strong. But I wanted people to know that I was really weak; I wanted someone to break through that and say, "Hey, I love you as a weak person. I care about you and you don't have to play this game with me anymore." But no one ever did.

Let me backtrack a little. A few years before the breakdown I started keeping a journal. I was fourteen when I started. The journal was a very private space for me. It's when I could talk about hurt and anger. I could talk about depression. A lot of it was about the pressure I was under, the terror. I was terrified of being alone. I couldn't handle it, and I think what I did was write it down so that on reading it back I wasn't alone. I could make my records come alive in that journal. I could say that Paul Simon wrote this and Paul Simon is my friend because he knows that. And I thought it, and on reading my writing of it, there was someone else saying the same thing to me. So it was that confirmation that I wasn't really alone, because I was terrified of that.

I was depressed at the time. No one ever picked up on it. I kept saying, "My God, look at how fucked up I am. Look at how lonely I am. Look at how scared I am. Why doesn't anyone ever bother to tell me anything? Why doesn't anyone ever see this?" I thought I had given people signs — I don't think everyone runs around telling people they're going to die at twenty-two. I wasn't overtly depressed. I would never cry in public; I would always go to my room. I was never *in* public. That was part of it. I went to school, came home, and went to my room. At nine o'clock homework was over so I watched television for two hours and went to bed. I was a perfect child, according to my mother. I remember one day I wrote in the journal, "This is a perfect child," and just put a big question mark and then ripped the page in half. I felt someone had to be really stupid to think that I was perfect: "Why are all these people so blind?" you know. "What's wrong with me? Why can't people see? They should care enough to find out what I'm like. *I* care enough; I'm sensitive to people. *I* know where they're at. Why doesn't someone ever do that to me? Where is that person?" The only people I could find were in my music.

My style of writing was very self-conscious and precocious. I would figure, "If someone cares about me, they're going to follow my thoughts. I'm going to put them in the order I think them." There was no coherent order. I think someone reading it would find it incredibly confusing. I left sign-posts here and there. I would do things like, "If this is confusing to you, check this out," so I was obviously writing it hoping that someday someone would read it. If I had made a deliberate attempt to kill myself I would have left a note saying, "Look at my journals" because it would be the only thing about me that would last. And it would be my last plea for people to be kind, to be gentle, and to love other people – to finally have someone listen to the message.

They were my last attempt to reach out to people. I'm aware that I was willing to sacrifice my life if that would make people listen.

The music that really got to me was the Jefferson Airplane. They were sort of the vanguard of political rock, acid rock, in the United States. Their second album – "Surrealistic Pillow" – talked a lot about the right to have love everywhere, and that fitted exactly what I needed. I needed love and never got it. There were a lot of drug allusions, and that's just when I was getting into drugs and hiding it from my parents, and getting spaced out in front of the stereo all the time. My mother hated them. And they meant something to me. They were saying, "Yes, it's right to believe in love and to realize that you don't get it in this world and they should change it. And if you need drugs to escape from this world that's the thing to do." That message comes across really clearly. I took my cue from that. I said, "Okay. This is the world I want, the world of beauty and love, and I guess what they're saying is true." Well it got to the point where I was heavily into drugs. For about two or three months there I was doing two trips a day on acid.

There was this girl in college, Beth, whom I really cared for. Just before the breakdown I wrote her a long, rambling, desperate letter. I told her that if I didn't make it through the breakdown I would kill myself, and I wanted my death to mean something. I gave her all the instructions for my funeral: the songs to play, the poetry, excerpts from books to read; that I wanted my friends there, and I wanted my friends to burn me and then plant flowers with my ashes because then something would grow and I hope other people would understand. Down to every last detail. Because it was really critical to me that if I didn't make it, that I could communicate by my failure what I was trying to achieve, so that maybe the people at the funeral could learn from it.

That made the whole thing sensible to me. That gave me the courage to try it, to try my breakdown. To say, "If I succeed, great for me. If I fail, great for everyone else. Whatever happens there will be a meaning to it, a good purpose; either way it will lead to love." Which is what I had to know before I started. I couldn't think of trying it, and I would never have gone on that risky a journey, unless I knew that either way would lead to my goal — for people to love each other. When I start talking about it I still get really emotional, because it's still really hard. Sometimes I still feel frustrated that the message just doesn't get around.

Anyway, Beth got the letter and she came down and said, "I know and understand what's going on and I care about you and I want you with me." She physically moved me to her place. I think if she hadn't done that I very well might have said, "This is silly. I can't communicate with anyone. I might as well give it up and try the one thing that people cannot ignore." Because people can't ignore a dead body; they've got to do something with it. I really think that's very critical for someone in that type of situation; so often they're going to keep trying to communicate, and all they need is that one person to listen.

I was lucky. I had a good psychiatrist. I did two years of

really hard work and for the first time in my life, often I'm happy. And that means more to me, I think, than anything. I can feel sad now and not feel desperate. I can feel put down by people and finally recover from that. I don't have to be belligerent against all people in the world. My parents were very supportive when I was ready to put myself back together. When I was into drugs there wasn't much they could do for me because I didn't want to communicate with them. I was deliberately shutting them out because I felt they had rejected me, when in fact they hadn't. They are just cool, rational people who didn't know what to do with me. We really get along well now. They always cared.

I still have trouble dealing with anger, though. I can't come right out and say to a person, "Look, something you did really hurt me." I try to lay guilt trips on them like my mother did to me. But I'm learning. Now I'm really in the sun. Things are great. And I'm trying to fill some of the needs in people that I needed to be filled myself. And that's what I want to end up doing. I sensed in my own life how important that is. You don't have to be a professional to do that first bit, to just listen and respond. You just have to be a human being who cares about another human being.

Diane

I'd look at everyone around me and feel different and crazy. I was peculiar. I never thought anyone would fall in love with me or that I could love someone. The only living thing I really cared for was my horse.

It wasn't always like that though. When I was little things were pretty good. I have two brothers who are quite a bit older than I am, so I'm the baby of the family. I was always very pampered and fussed over. But I was lonely because my brothers were so much older and never around, so I was like an only child. I used to have to rummage through my friends and ask them to come along when I went somewhere with my parents. I always wanted a sister or just a companion. The best day of the week was Sunday. That was the day I spent with my father. I always got along just super with him and still do.

By the time I was twelve I started not getting along with my mother. She just didn't know what to do with a girl. My brothers were really rowdy and she was afraid I'd be like them so she was too strict at first. I'd be really bad. My dad would always be on my side. She was also very jealous of me because my father had such a passion for me. She said that I got everything and she got nothing. My dad didn't get involved because he doesn't like waves. He'd let my mom go on and on. He didn't like to cause a fight or take an active role in front of my mother. He tried not to interfere, but they used to fight constantly about me.

When I was thirteen I got a horse. I was totally devoted to him. He was all I really cared about. I'd spend all my weekends with him. My mother never encouraged my interest in the horse. She complained about having to take me to the stable. She wanted me to live up to what she wanted. She encouraged ballet and piano and stuff that I had no talent for. I thought of going into nursing, and when I changed my mind she was angry. Then I thought I might want to learn to be a riding teacher. They had an insurance policy that was supposed to pay for my education. She said, "No. If you're going to do that we're not paying. I'm going to take that money and it's going to be mine." All because I'm not doing what she wants me to do, right?

I always had a lot of friends, but my best friends always seemed to turn into my worst friends. I got tired of them or we'd have a fight. I found it hard to maintain friends that I could be close to for a long time. I took it personally.

When I was fifteen I started to get very introverted. I'd go out with boys, but I was never very popular. They'd talk to me like I was one of the boys. One of my friends was absolutely gorgeous. She'd get guys interested in her and then drop them. Whenever I was interested in a guy, she'd deliberately go after him and then drop him after she got him. That alienated me from these boys, because I was her best friend so they were embarrassed to talk to me after.

I really started to get very introverted around Christmas. I wouldn't go with my parents to visit relatives. I just sat around. I wouldn't eat. I was full of self-pity. I didn't like myself at all. Maybe I didn't want to see people because I didn't think I was presentable. I just had a feeling of badness about myself. I'd go to my bedroom after supper and stay up there all night every night. I had no one to talk to about it. I'd just pound on my typewriter. I'd write long compositions about what was bothering me.

I think I felt so bad about myself because I hadn't accomplished anything I was proud of. I never did anything special. I didn't even feel normal. I went out with this fellow, but as soon as he really liked me I couldn't continue the relationship. We'd go to a show and then he'd want to go for pizza, and I'd say, "Oh, no. You can't spend all that money on me." I didn't think I was worth spending money on. I broke up with him and introduced him to a friend, and they started going out. I was so reclusive. I didn't want to be alone but forced myself to be. I was trying to get people to notice that something was wrong and I needed help. Either people are uncomfortable with it or they slough it off.

Once I made myself up to look like I was dead for a week. I put white powder on my face. Nobody said anything. I was trying to get them to notice. I talked to them once and said, "Look, there's something wrong with me." I'd go out with my friends and literally just stare for hours and not say a word. I just wanted someone to notice. It became a habit. I wanted someone to say, "What's wrong." No one asked. I was trying to show people that something was wrong with my head.

I once submitted some death poetry to a teacher; he said it was a selfish, morbid poem. He said it was one sided. I mean, he was really critical of it. Those were my feelings. I was hurting and he was being critical of my feelings! I couldn't see anything getting better.

My mother noticed that something was wrong. She'd try to

help, but I'd just push her away. When she couldn't get through to me she'd say, "Oh you're so miserable and rotten and ugly. No wonder you don't have any friends." That made it worse. I was vulnerable at that time and believed it. I lived up to the expectations she had of me. I never thought of going to my father with my problems because I didn't want to burden him.

Well the last straw came with my horse. I loved him so much because he gave me no critical feedback and he was always there when I needed him. One Sunday I came out to ride him and he had died. At that point every bit of life drained out of me. It was an explosion in my head. I wouldn't cry in front of everyone; I went into the barn and I cried my heart out. I went to my friend's house and cried a bit; then I went home. My parents went out, but I didn't want to go with them. They didn't want to leave me alone. The horse had been the only thing I ever found that I could really care for, and I screwed that up, too. I felt somehow responsible because I hadn't been riding that much. I had neglected him — that was the only thing I'd really done well.

Then I got to thinking that whenever I seemed to get close to something it died. I was an animal lover. I had a cat. I got super close to it and it died. I had another cat I was close to and it died under the wheel of my father's car. He didn't tell me. I hadn't fed it one day and I thought the cat ran away; I felt guilty because I hadn't fed it. For a whole summer I went looking for it every night on my bicycle. Once I brought home a cat that looked absolutely nothing like my cat. It was a stray cat and really wild. It scratched the hell out of me. I convinced myself it was Tiger and he had just gone nuts. Finally after a year my mother told me. I'd felt guilty for a whole year.

And my grandmother, I'd just gotten close to her and she died. I was about five; she got a brain tumour. I used to visit her every day. It affected me because — my mom didn't mean it, but I told her that one day when I was visiting her she was bumping into things and she spilled her tea. My mother said, "Why didn't you tell someone?" I didn't know I was supposed to. I did everything wrong, and felt guilty.

So I went downstairs. I shoved everything into my mouth — my mother's nerve pills and Seconal sleeping pills — and swallowed them with water. I wanted to die, and I got paranoid. I thought what if I haven't taken enough? What happens if I'm just a vegetable and can't even do this right? So I phoned the distress centre and said I was scared I hadn't taken enough, and was just going to be a vegetable. They said, "Oh, no. You're going to die," and I said, "Oh, good." They offered to send someone to get me to a hospital. I said no, there's no reason for me to live. I had no purpose, absolutely no purpose in life. I started getting drowsier and drowsier and the guy said, "You don't really want to die." I said, "Yeah." As I started to get drowsier he started to wear me down a bit and then I got to the point where I wasn't so proud. At first I didn't want to fail in this. After a while that wore off and I said, "Okay." But I didn't want them to pick me up in front of my house. I said to pick me up on the corner. I called my friend and told her what I did, and she came right down. I was out on the lawn on a corner lot and I was starting to feel really good; really peaceful. It felt good to feel so peaceful. Then I started to change my mind and wanted to die. It would be a good thing to feel like this all the time. I told my friend and she was really upset. Finally the guy came and picked me up.

When I woke up the next morning my mother was there. I went home. I didn't want to go home. I didn't want to be the same person. I wanted to be a totally new person. I wanted to go to a new school and have new friends. I said, "Next time it's not going to be pills. It's going to be a knife or a gun." I wished I'd never gone to the hospital. People were bombarding me. My mother felt guilty. My brother and sister-in-law and my other brother invited me to live with them. The man at the stable where I had my horse said he had a new horse that I'd really like and invited me to stay with them for two weeks. I caused all these problems and made everyone scared and paranoid. Things weren't getting better in my head. It was just getting worse.

Then my friend's boyfriend came over and straightened out my whole head. He said I was so good and I had so much to live for. He told me he liked me. I felt really inferior and all my friends were really pretty. He said, "You have four times the personality of all of them and twice the brains. You have so much to live for. It's such a fantastic world."

I was so happy and so hyper. Everything was great. I remember a month later at the circus, I was so happy that I started crying because I was actually there and happy and I could have missed all that.

After the suicide attempt I got into drama. There was this part that wasn't for me. I couldn't act, but the teacher turned down two other girls that wanted the part because he knew I was having problems and really needed it. Then my mother got me an appointment with a psychiatrist. He was a child psychologist and didn't know how to deal with an adolescent. He was weird. He said have you ever done drugs and I said no. "Have you ever had sex?" I said "No." And he said, "Why? Hasn't anyone ever asked you?" I said, "Yes, but I never liked anyone enough." So he asked if I was frigid. I told him about this dream I had that my friend was locking all my friends in a closet and hanging and killing them. And he said, "Why are you afraid that your mother is going to find out that you're queer?" I thought, "Oh, great. This guy is more screwed up than I am."

It was very reassuring to have all those people show how much they really cared about me after my suicide attempt. My parents and my friends were super. It's bad that I had to have them prove it, and yet I didn't do it to get them to prove to me that they cared. I didn't expect the reaction I got. I didn't know people would be so hurt if I wasn't around.

But despite all that I wasn't finished with suicide yet. Three years later when I thought I was really okay I started going out with this guy who loved me, but I knew he wasn't for me. I had to get out of the relationship, and then I started to regress. He was hurt and bitter. He'd call me names in front of others when he was drunk. I'd try to ignore it, but I started to believe what he said and my opinion of myself got lower and lower. It reached a head when I thought I wasn't worth anything. He blew my ego. I actually walked into a store and bought razor blades. What prevented me from using them was the knowledge that things had gotten better before so they had to get better again. It was something I went through and I learned from it. I stopped dwelling on everything bad and started looking at the good.

Since that time I've been fine and I would never let it happen again. I know myself better than I ever have. If someone tells me I have a funny nose — well, that's fine, but I have terrific eyes. I know myself now so if they say something negative, well, fine. I have enough confidence and maybe I've gotten to like myself and not think of myself as a totally bad person.

I know now that part of growing up is realizing that there are good times and bad times. It's simply a matter of putting up with the bad times till things get better. They always do. And everyone goes through the stage where they really doubt their self worth. I'm sure it's simply part of growing up, too.

Now if I had a serious problem I wouldn't stay home and mope about it. I would get out and do things. I would work a lot of overtime. I'd sit and listen to my friends' problems. I'd worry about others. I'd list my assets against my debits. My assets win. I really haven't had a tough life. I have an apartment, furniture, and a good job. I'm lucky that I have a healthy body and mind. Suicide is an intensely self-centred phenomenon. You aren't thinking about anyone except yourself.

I wasn't crazy. My suicide attempt was a plea for someone to listen and tell me where I was going and why I was here. I had no purpose. My parents tried to give it to me but they couldn't get through. I wouldn't let them close. Everyone thought the problem was my mother — but it wasn't. It was me — the way I viewed things; the way I reacted. I just blew everything up out of all proportion. When I look back at what happened I look back at a totally different person. I can't believe that was me.

I'm not the only one who's gotten better. My whole family has. I was a really disruptive force between my parents. Now they're cuddly and loving again the way they used to be. And my brothers and I are very close. I feel really good about myself.

In our society we like to put labels on stages of human development – terrible twos, fearsome fours, troubled teens, male menopause. We do it because labels provide us with certain expectations so that we know how to proceed. We have an immediate handle to grab for understanding.

Troubled teens means that adolescence is viewed as a period of turmoil. No less an authority than Anna Freud sees adolescence as an expectable transitional phase of upset between the relatively stable psychological worlds of childhood and adult life.[1] Certainly, adolescence is not an easy time because it's a period of social, physical, and intellectual transformation. The world of childhood, with its security and lack of responsibility, is left behind; the world of the adult beckons, but admission is not yet granted. The adolescent's body suddenly develops so that he resembles an adult and has the sexual longings of an adult; but he doesn't have the emotional maturity to deal with these longings, and adult society has dictated that he has to wait. He also becomes eager to try out new values and ideas. Equality, justice, love, and truth now take on serious significance, but they can be overwhelming. Through it all the teenager is trying to find and define himself.

One psychiatrist paints this picture of the adolescent:

There comes to mind the melancholic-bitter brooding of the young adolescent, self-doubting, disoriented by the change he perceives in himself and in his environment, disappointed at not being more than he is, just at the time he thought he was becoming an adult. Because of the tormenting feeling of inadequacy, he begins to turn inward on himself, to burn his bridges, to break off contacts in order to spare himself defeats. He does not understand himself, and he feels misunderstood ... insofar as he doubts himself, he affirms himself noisily in an arrogant and aggressive manner

73

... To be himself, to affirm himself in his new status, he must get away from and differentiate himself from all that has to do with his old status ... [2]

Professional literature is filled with similar descriptions portraying teenagers as erratic, unstable, troublesome creatures. To be sure, many indeed do fit the description, and a psychiatrist's perspective may be coloured by the fact that almost all the adolescents he sees are troubled. But for a parent to unquestioningly assimilate this view of adolescence can be damaging. For example, two young parents were discussing the virtues of their extremely well-behaved and intelligent four-year-old daughter. Suddenly, the husband turned to his wife and said, "We'd better enjoy her now because we're sure to have grief from her when she's a teenager." These parents could be inviting trouble, because children often live up to the expectations – good or bad – that their parents have of them.

Labels are destructive in another way. As psychiatrist James Anthony puts it, they can cause parents "to respond to their adolescent children as if they were embodiments of negative ideas rather than real people."[3] If a son is moody, depressed and withdrawn, the best-intentioned parents might be inclined not to take it too seriously because they could rationalize that it's just a "stage." Meanwhile, the son may be so desperate for attention in his plight that he might be entertaining thought of suicide. Alternatively, parents might be inclined to overreact to their teenager's behaviour. If a sixteen-year-old girl is an hour late getting home from a date, her mother might be furious with her and accuse her of immoral behaviour, because that's what teenage girls do when they stay out late. The daughter, who may have done no more than forget the time, may feel rage or guilt or worthlessness at her mother's sudden violent outburst. The mother, whose only motive was to protect and discipline, may have made the situation worse by alienating her daughter – at least temporarily – and driving home to her the message that her mother doesn't understand her or respect her. So much for labels.

What makes adolescence so difficult, but at the same time

such a potentially rewarding period, is that it is a time of testing, both for parents and children. The young person tests out the adult role he will play later – like a dress rehearsal for adulthood. Vital issues like "How do I handle problems?", "How do I relate to other people?", "How do I view myself?", "How do I feel about my parents?" – in short, "Who am I?" and "Am I worthy?" have to be confronted. For parents it's a time of testing too. "Have we done a good job with our child?", "Do we like what we see emerging into adulthood?", "Does our child love us?" and "Are we worthy in his eyes?" are some of the questions they want answered. Ultimately, the true measure of success is for the parents to be able to let go, and for the young person to be able to take what he has learned from his parents and emerge as an adult – as intact as possible.

Howard's story illustrates that feelings of love and concern from parents aren't enough to create a happy, stable child who can manage difficult times and who can create sustaining relations with others. The feeling of love for a child, in the abstract, comes easily and naturally enough for most parents. But to be able to say to a child, "I love you for what you are, not for what I want you to be. I love you with your weaknesses, your fears, and all your imperfections; despite them you are a special person" – to have and express that feeling of love in the particular requires certain parenting skills. Sadly, not enough parents have them. And not for lack of trying.

Howard is locked into a role he's not suited to play, and his parents have thrown away the key. They expect him to be strong and independent because that is a family tradition. The fact that he can't meet these expectations makes him feel guilty. Although he hasn't been taught how to play that role, in his eyes, and in his parents' eyes, he has failed. He can't express his failure because to do so would be an acknowledgement of weakness which is unacceptable in view of the family tradition. The free expression of emotion isn't encouraged, as *that's* not part of the tradition, either. It's a circular problem that will eventually tighten itself around Howard in a grip of death.

Sure his parents have told him that he's terrific and can do anything he wants to do. Then why doesn't he fight back when he's bullied? Why does he allow his friend to lie to him? Why does he continue to tolerate a situation that is intolerable? Because he feels he deserves all that abuse. He's a weakling and a failure. They are his just rewards.

We can imagine the courage it takes – and the intense pain Howard suffers – to tell his parents that he can't handle the situation in school. But instead of giving him sympathy, assurance, and help, his parents decide to send him to military school. Howard views this as rejection, motivated by shame and disappointment. We know that his parents make that decision for what they no doubt interpret as his best interests: They see him as weak and they want to toughen him up, in Davis fashion. This is their way of helping him.

Howard's parents are mortally afraid of failure, as he so astutely tells us. If he requires psychiatric help, then he is weak and they have not been good parents. They interpret his suicide attempt in the same light, and to a certain extent, they are right. Through his suicide attempt he does reproach his parents for having rejected him. Unlike Doreen and Bill in Chapter One, his attempt is not carried out with the intention of punishing or manipulating people. He does it because it is a logical outcome of the way he sees himself. "If no one wants me, I don't want myself." He is unworthy and deserves to die.

Another aspect of his parents' failure is their inability to cope on an emotional level. We see this in the way his mother handles anger, but it is especially clear in their reaction to his suicide attempt. Instead of rushing to his side in an effort to make a new beginning, instead of saying, "Let's all work together and help each other," they are too caught up in *their* own inadequacies and *their* own reactions. They are not selfish; they are powerless. Their "Why didn't you tell us?" is pathetic, because it indicates that they cannot respond to their son in the way he needs to be responded to. Nothing is solved by that question, and the problem remains untouched.

Howard's attempt at communicating with his parents, even through attempting suicide, has failed. Neither he nor his parents can express what they really want to say. His parents have applied the family label to him, and can view him only in terms of those artificial expectations, which he does not meet. By those standards he *is* a failure, regardless of his other achievements. The standards they establish have importance only for them. To force them on Howard is to reduce his worth. To label is to disable.[4]

We have already seen the devastating effects of setting goals that don't take the child into account in Bill's story in Chapter One. His father expected him to go to a particular university, to play on the football team, and to get a degree. It didn't matter that Bill was a talented musician who had no hankering for his father's dreams. If he didn't live the way his father wanted him to, then his father condemned him as a failure. Bill adopted his father's standards, saw himself as a failure, and spent years recklessly testing himself and proving himself worthless through the suicidal pursuits of alcohol and drugs.

Howard, too, is labelled "failure." If he can't find an affirmation of himself through his family or friends, he will fabricate it through images and songs that speak directly to him. But the device that most strongly fills that need for comfort is, of course, his journal. In it he reveals the "weak" side of himself that he can reveal nowhere else, and so he unburdens himself somewhat. Certainly, his journal is intensely egocentric; that is its purpose. Paul Osterrieth, writing of adolescents who keep journals, says, "He [the adolescent] thus reveals the attention he pays to himself and the consciousness he has of the passage of time and of his progression towards a new stage."[4] But the new stage that Howard progresses to is death.

Certainly we know that Howard is depressed. In an effort to draw attention to that fact, he publicly commits himself to death before the age of twenty-two. What he promises, simply, is that he will never live to adulthood. He will kill himself soon. He perverts the code of honour with which his family has imbued him. He says he's dying so that people can recognize love in the world, but what he really wants is for people to love him. Howard confuses self-love with global love. He's begging for someone to discover that he's weak and mortal, and to save him. He's testing to see if anyone cares enough about him to save him. In that testing there is an inherent optimism. A. Alvarez tells us that, "if suicide is a cry for help, then the young, even in their self-destruction, remain optimistic . . . They still believe that something or someone will turn up."[6]

Howard is fortunate. Not only does Beth respond to his test in a way that no human being has ever responded to him before – totally, sincerely, and with no strings attached – but he also gives himself a last minute chance by deciding to attempt a breakdown first.

He brings about this mental breakdown by taking LSD twice a day for two or three months. He wants to break himself down so that he can put himself back together again. The result is, in a sense, a rebirth; the breakdown, then, is a death or sorts – a modified suicide. Howard is not unique in his motives for his breakdown-suicide. Says Alvarez:

> There is, I believe, a whole class of suicides, who take their own lives not in order to die, but in order to escape confusion, to clear their heads. They deliberately use suicide to create an unencumbered reality for themselves or to break through the patterns of obsession and necessity which they have unwittingly imposed on their lives.[7]

The obsessions that Howard can now discard are his promise of an early death – he can still live with honour – and his perceived failure. At least his breakdown has been successful.

We are glad that Howard has gone through his terrible ordeal and has put himself back together. As we shall see in Chapter Five, to rejoice for Howard is to have a heightened sense of the futility of Peter's death. He could have made it too, if only someone had listened, if only he hadn't been so proud, if only, if only . . .

By now many of the elements of Diane's story are so familiar to us that they begin to sound like an old refrain: the discord with a parent, feelings of worthlessness, unsuccessful attempts at communicating those feelings, the destructive powers of anger and guilt, and suicide as a way out. That we have heard them all before, doesn't diminish their intrinsic worth in any way; it merely emphasizes that as human beings we all have certain basic needs and responses, and perhaps suicidal individuals feel them more strongly.

One big problem in Diane's young teenage life is her mother, because as far as her mother is concerned the nubile Diane is now The Other Woman. She is a rival for her husband's affections and she appears to be winning. This is not an unusual phenomenon. While a girl approaches adolescence, her mother approaches menopause. One's sexual allure is flowering while the other's is waning. As psychiatrist James Anthony puts it, "The interaction stirs up considerable anxiety and depression in both, and the relationship . . . is transformed into an open warfare in which the Geneva conventions are abandoned. The father often carries a 'diplomatic immunity' in these situations."[8]

This is clearly an unfair situation for any mother to find herself in. Her daughter repays her for all her nurturing not only by cutting her mother off from her affections, but by betraying her with the man she loves, her husband. Diane's mother feels shut out. Her anger simmers. In the face of Diane's "typical teenage behaviour" it explodes. Diane is moody and depressed. When her mother – who is a genuinely concerned parent despite the squabbles – tries to reach out to her daughter to help her, she is met with cold, irritating rejection. When her overtures of goodwill are rejected, she can no longer contain her anger. Her furious words are indicative of her own frustration because she is powerless to deal with the situation; but she makes it sound as if Diane is the shabby villain. Because Diane is so vulnerable, she picks up the message and uses it as a mirror in which she views herself. She is bad and ugly.

We can't blame Diane for thwarting her mother's efforts to help her. We can guess that her mother must have lashed out at her before in blind anger. She fears that she may be emotionally assaulted again. Rather than risk it, Diane prefers to keep things to herself. Her mother's brutal anger has driven a heavy wedge between them.

Like Bill's and Howard's parents, Diane's mother (her father is so passive that we get no feeling for him at all) has certain expectations of her daughter that don't take Diane's wishes into account. Parents who do that only want what's best for their children; but they also try to live vicariously through them, and they deprive them of the opportunity to assume the responsibility for the direction of their lives. It means disregarding their children as people in their own right, and that, as we know, is hurtful.

Another aspect of Diane's development that proves to be troublesome is her experience with death. From childhood on, death has never been properly explained to her. Most people feel some guilt when a person or even a pet close to them dies, but because the issue wasn't dealt with openly in Diane's family, no one ever allayed her guilt. She felt that she was singlehandedly responsible for those deaths that occurred when she was a very impressionable child, and was hardly equipped to deal with the implications of death. The death of her horse, which has become the sole object of her affections, comes at a time when she feels particularly unhappy with herself. It doesn't take much for her to conclude that she is the cause of her horse's death. If she could let all those deaths happen and if she is such a bad human being, then she deserves to die herself.

The fact that Diane doesn't like herself is reflected not only in the way she deals with and views her relationships with her mother and animals, but also in the way she defines relationships with her friends. She deliberately sets up situations that are designed to humiliate and defeat her. In choosing a girlfriend who will constantly betray and outclass her, she reveals that she doesn't have very much self-confidence. This same lack of self-confidence makes it impossible for Diane to stand up for herself. We can only guess that she must have tried to develop other friendships among similar negative lines. Because she has such a poor self-image she has no difficulty in convincing herself that she was responsible for all her failed relationships.

Like most of the people we have met so far, Diane gives strong indications that she is suicidal. She is depressed and withdrawn. She writes death poetry and submits it to her teacher. (She is actually reprimanded for expressing selfish feelings!) She even goes so far as to try to fashion a death mask for herself. All her attempts go unnoticed, or to be more precise, they are noticed, but as Diane says, "Either people are uncomfortable with it or they try to slough it off." Nobody reaches out to her until *after* her suicide attempt. She, too, is testing her own worth, not manipulating or punishing. All she wants is for one person to say to her, "I care for you just the way you are."

It is significant that, like Lenore and Howard and thousands of other teenagers, Diane's suicide attempt is made with tranquillizers and sleeping pills belonging to a parent and found abundantly in the house. Parents who need to make life more bearable for themselves by using large amounts of these pills often succeed in making suicide easy for their children.

Fortunately for Diane, her suicide attempt brings people to her side – her psychiatrist notwithstanding – so that she can put herself back together. Like Howard she was hoping that her suicide would serve as an opportunity for rebirth, an occasion to leave the old hated self behind and emerge a new person. But the trick, of course, is to learn to live with the old person. To do that Diane has come to accept certain truths about herself at her particular stage of life: that as an adolescent she tended to blow things up out of all proportion and so make them worse than they actually were, that as an adolescent she lacked the cumulative experience to recognize that bad times don't last forever. Good times come eventually. And she has come to know that she has strengths that she can rely on. Diane's testing has shown her not only that others can love her, but that she can love herself. She is a valuable human being who can survive.

Howard and Diane are fortunate that people rushed to their

rescue to help them live. How much better if they had had the self-confidence and self-esteem to weather crises in a way that would have helped them grow, rather than making them wish to destroy themselves. Surely the challenge to parents is to inspire love, growth and life in their children, and to assure that their children will not have to resort to laying their lives on the line to test their parents' love. When parents fail this test, they invite their children's self-destruction.

4

COLOUR ME GAY

Dear Mama

...I have something to tell you that I guess I better not put off any longer.... You see, I am a homosexual. I have fought it off for months and maybe years, but it just grows truer. I have never yet had an actual affair with anybody, I give you my word on that, not even Pete, whom I suppose you will think of right away because we room together and go places together....

I know how much pain this will cause you, and shock too. But I can't keep it a secret from you any longer.... Again, I'm terribly sorry to give you this shock and pain, but that's the way it is...

Laura Z. Hobson, Consenting Adult

Bruce

I contemplated suicide for long periods of time. This goes back five years ago. There was a series of events that led to a depression. It started in grade ten. I had started in a new senior high school, and I found it kind of traumatic. Not the work — it was something like a culture shock. I was coming from a small junior high. I felt lost in a big crowd. I started having tummy aches and finding it very hard to get up in the morning. I also had severe allergies and this made it even harder to get up in the mornings. I was getting depressed, but I was also physically sick at the same time which greatened the burden.

Up until this time I was an A student, very good in school, very well behaved. I came home one day and had a horrible migraine headache. The pain was unreal and I was crying. My parents rushed me to the hospital and I was there for a week of tests – brain scans and things. I guess I was trying to tell my parents that something wasn't right. It was my way of communicating that.

Finally I was released from the hospital and they suggested that I get into a children's psychiatric ward. I was fifteen at the time. It was the biggest waste of time; I was pumped full of tranquillizers for four weeks, and saw this doctor whom I wouldn't cross the street to spit on right now. The only thing he could believe was that every fifteen-year-old boy had to be on drugs. If I still sound kind of bitter right now it's because I am bitter. He was a know-it-all. I might have been only fifteen, but I was a pretty in-tune kid.

So that ended abruptly. I was released from the hospital. My parents took two months off and we went down to Florida. Then it was summer and suddenly everything was okay. My parents really cared about me all the way through.

Came fall and once again I started into grade ten. This time I went right through until February and once again I became depressed. I was starting to feel bad and staying in bed for two, three, four days. I got into a drop-in program at the hospital. It was like a big community club. And then summer came and I was okay again. Summer seems to have some kind of magic effect on me. But the thing I found bad about that program was the staff. They were in their early twenties handling kids who were fifteen, sixteen, seventeen, and a lot of the staff didn't have it all together. It didn't work out too well.

The idea of bombing out of grade ten twice was getting me down too. I had always been a good student. This time my parents suggested a private school. Once again I zilched out about December. I stayed out a couple of months but I was able to make it up and get through that year.

Then it was on to grade eleven. I transferred schools again in mid-year. Because I had been in a psychiatric ward there was a stigma attached to it. I tended to be greatly over-sensitive, and a lot of kids at that age can be pretty cruel. I would tend to drop people and change friends. I would be kind of rootless.

I guess what I'm trying to do is to give you an overview of a depression that was happening. There were a lot of reasons for it. I had been overprotected and pretty sheltered at home. I don't blame my parents for it; they were really good. But I think maybe there is a point of overprotection. I never had a summer job till I was nineteen. Every time I'd think of getting a summer job my dad would raise my allowance. I think I was very lucky, but I think they might have encouraged me to work.

My older brother was going through medical school and he was giving my parents a hard time. They were giving him most of the attention. That was too bad in a way because I felt that I could've used it then, at the start of it. I'm not trying to blame them, but that's one way of looking at it.

One way of coping with my depression was to zonk myself out on tranquillizers. I had quite a supply around that my psychiatrist had given me. My parents used to go away quite a bit for the weekends and things. So I'd put myself out for four or five days. I never did myself any damage. I knew what I was doing. I would set my alarm for every four hours, take a pill, and go back to sleep. To me it was a way of escaping. Usually I'd come to terms with reality after a few days. I'd get up and get dressed. I was pretty lucky that my parents took a lot of holidays. That couldn't have happened if they were at home. Nobody was really around to check on me.

I've been avoiding it all along because I didn't know how you'd react, but the real big factor in my depressions was my sexual identity.

I first knew I was gay because guys seemed more important to me. I seemed to make friends easier with girls, but a guy friend was more important. Physical attraction played the most important role. I enjoyed it too much to let it frighten me. But after making bad contacts with gay people I went back to girls. Sort of like a yo-yo.

At the time I hadn't been able to communicate this, and the responses I had gotten every time I tried just freaked me right out. I tried once to tell my psychiatrist and he just ignored me. That would have been a great time for an in-tune therapist to have reached out for me because I would have been willing, but it was still hard for me. The second time I chose a male psychiatric nurse who was gay himself. He was basically an unstable person and worried that his job would be in danger. His response really threw me, and I became afraid to reach out again.

Everything I knew about the gay community at the time really scared me. There was no one I could see who was leading a positive life. I don't really know if I saw myself as being sick in that sense, but I definitely felt that I wasn't normal. That really upset me.

I coped with the problem by heading in the opposite direction. I've always been fairly comfortable with girls. So to prove my masculinity I became a mover in the school.

I didn't tell my parents, though I think I could have because they're both fine artists and had worked with a lot of gay people. It wasn't even that I didn't want to hurt them. I was just so wrapped up in myself that it didn't even occur to me. I was just into trying to figure out the whole matter for myself and I was intent on doing it. I guess it was my bad experiences with the hospital, though I can't say for sure.

Maybe, too, I didn't feel close enough to my parents to tell them. It's a neat way of avoidance, too. It's the normal adolescent alienation.

My lover and I were having a lot of problems in our relationship. I'm afraid I was out of control; this was the biggie. I was completely overwhelmed by depression. I would get so that it would take me a day to get up and wash my face. I'd start crying a lot in the afternoon by myself. My lover and I lived in a little apartment downtown and he was away at work during the day.

A lot of things were happening then. The relationship with my lover was falling apart. I was trying to get on Student Aid so I could go back to school, but my parents were pretty comfortable, and every time I went to ask for help they told me to move back home with my parents, and just about threw me out of the office. And then I found out that I had to have a spinal fusion. So everything happened at once.

I finally got into school, but I was so depressed I couldn't handle it. I had been an excellent student before, but now I couldn't even do fractions. That freaked me out even more. I eventually got so that one day I just walked out of school babbling and hallucinating. I walked into this mental health place, and they finally talked me down and sent me to a doctor. He didn't realize the state of my depression. He just put me on anti-depressant pills and let me go back to what was happening. I think he just thought it was a phase.

My lover and I were both nineteen when we met. We both dropped out of school, but we were both very unskilled in the way of having a relationship. Any relationships we'd had before had always been on very superficial levels. We had a lot of pressure on us from friends who wanted us to jump back into school – don't ruin your lives or don't do this. Both sets of our parents didn't know. We were smothering each other. Basically we both really loved each other at the time, and still do; but that got lost beneath everything else. Especially the smothering part. I had lost contact with so many people, and for me people are very important.

The money situation was horrible. For the first time in my life I was desperately poverty stricken. I'd never known this. Wow, what a shock! I'd gone on welfare for a while and that was the most degrading, horrible experience in my entire life. It certainly didn't do much for my self-esteem. But I wasn't ready to pack it all in. I could've moved back home any time I wanted to and had use of two cars, a big bedroom, and three warm meals a day; but I wasn't ready for that.

In the big depression I had a constant death wish. I'd be lying around in bed, but my brain would be hopping at ninety-five miles an hour. I was like a hamster running on a wheel. I was too passive to even initiate anything like killing myself. I just lay around and wished for death all day.

My parents finally stepped in. They took me to a hospital where I was hospitalized for a couple of weeks. Once again I had a bad experience with a doctor there. Homosexuality bothered him terribly.

But then good things started to happen that helped to get me out of that depression. I unexpectedly came into some money, which helped to relieve our poverty. I started seeing a really good therapist who didn't pick up where anyone else had left off, but she started for the first time. I also got Student Aid. It seemed that one pressure after another was lifted. It certainly wasn't from any magical treatment that I received from any doctors. When the outside pressures were alleviated it put me in a space to look at what was happening. With me working through my therapist and with my lover wanting to work at it too, there was real communication. I went back to school and he went into an interior decorating program. So we started developing outside interests that are so important. Basically we started developing more people contacts. And the possessiveness went away because we felt more secure about each other. It happened gradually and we really had to work at it.

My parents seemed to put too much trust in the almighty doctor. And I think they were genuinely annoyed with me for chucking out one doctor after another. But then I was attending school and graduating. That made me really happy and increased my credibility with my parents. They've reacted very well to Steve and accept him as a son.

At fifteen I was living a lie, trying to prove my masculinity. But I didn't know I was doing it. In retrospect, it contributed to making me unhappy and depressed. I wasn't developing any healthy relationships. I didn't experience any physical things with girls then. With guys I had. I was choosing not to. But yet on the surface I had to be the man who was making it with the girls, because that's what I was out to prove.

My therapist was the first person who asked me if I was getting enough sleep. Very important. At the time I went into the hospital everyone told me that my perception was freaked up. That does wonders for you! She was the first one to say that I was doing all right under the circumstances. And she assured me that many psychiatrists are uncomfortable handling gay men. But you walk in there and you think that the man in the chair is able to handle that, and you just take this rejection onto yourself. You blame yourself. So I found out that it wasn't just me.

I was really on the brink of suicide and I've come back. I feel that to throw a fifteen-year-old into a den of lions – that psychiatric trip with all its pill-taking – that's just completely unreal. Why place so much faith in these doctors? I feel that, if I had had a different kind of program, a lot of pain and anguish for me could have been avoided.

The three doctors I went to just happened to be inadequate. The bad that they did far outweighed the good. None of them ever really dealt with my sexuality. It was almost like, "It's a stage you're going through. You'll get over it." They were chucking me aside. *Bop. Crash. Bop. Crash.*

I'm honest about it. If somebody asks me I'll tell them that I'm gay, but I don't go around advertising it. But I feel some kind of obligation to help other people who are gay. You shouldn't have to want to die because you're different.

Liz

There are two things that come to mind when I think of my family: religious and strict. They were fundamentalist in the Plymouth Brethren tradition. There were no movies, smoking, drinking, or dancing. Nothing except church three or four times a week. We were really lonely kids because we weren't allowed to hang around with anyone who didn't belong to my parents' immediate religious community. That cut us off from a whole lot of the world, as you can imagine.

My father didn't know how to handle his feelings; he was and is a depressed man. He's a classic, saying things like ''I won't be around much longer,'' ''you don't care about me,'' – doing all sorts of guilt numbers on us. It was really hard for young kids. We felt obliged to love him and look after him. The situation was really weird. You'd expect a parent at least once a year to say to a kid, I love you. But the direct question on more than one occasion was, Do you love me? Like really needing our love and our caring. We resented having to take care of him. I don't think we even knew how complicated our feelings were. My father was also an angry man, and he used to give my older brother and me frequent lickings whether we deserved it or not. I can remember saying shit once and getting beaten so hard that I was badly bruised. He used to whip off his belt and let us have it. I still think he got off on it.

From the way he was with us we learned a lot about how to be with yourself, by yourself. And that you didn't count. We were a very shy bunch of kids. I still feel that way sometimes. I still feel more inclined to withdraw from groups of people than to be involved. Sometimes I have to make an effort to be involved, and to talk with new people.

My mother didn't seem to feel that she had the power to intervene in any way, unfortunately. Even today I've tried to sit down with her to talk about how things were back then. And she has all sorts of guilt feelings on the way she raised us.

When I had problems I learned how to keep them inside. My family was not an open place to be. You didn't talk about problems in an open, problem-solving sort of way. Once in a while my mother would hug me.

I wasn't very old when she went out to bring in some extra money by looking after other people's kids, which was weird. Maybe she didn't care enough to stay at home and look after us.

My father treats guests in the home very differently from the way he treats his own kids. It just drives me nuts. He treats guests respectfully and will speak to them. He doesn't really talk to us.

By the time I got into my teens I was a very screwed-up kid. I was really, really lonely. That's a time more than any other time when there's pressure to be involved more with your peers and stuff. And I was really off to myself. It was hard for me to concentrate and to study. I did well in courses when the teacher took a personal interest in me. But in the others I couldn't be bothered. I never failed anything, but I wasn't what you call a top student. But I really put myself down a whole lot. My parents set up high expectations but never gave me the support or love to back that kind of thing up. And I wanted to live up to those expectations. I wanted my parents' approval and love. But it never really seemed to happen. I was pretty shy and introverted, and never felt that I belonged. I didn't want to hang around with kids from church anymore because I just wasn't into that. I really wanted to belong at school, but at the same time I felt guilty and too inadequate to become involved in any big way.

I wanted to become involved in sports – volleyball or basketball. Involvement that would mean acceptance and being liked. I also had one or two friends who were shy and studious. I fit in with them, but I had to keep putting limits on myself because my parents would disapprove if I got involved with them. I didn't date because there was a lot of pressure on us about that from my parents. It was just not okay.

I was totally unaware of my body. I remember one night, I was about twelve or thirteen, I woke up and was having really bad abdominal cramps. I went down to the bathroom and my mother woke up. When she saw what was happening she said, "Oh, I should have bought you napkins, I should have told you. You're going to have this from now on." But nothing positive and no real explanation. That's how I found out about menstruation.

When I found out about intercourse I couldn't imagine my parents doing it, partly because I thought it was dirty and partly because I knew there was supposed to be some pleasure involved. I couldn't believe that they could enjoy something and actually express affection.

My problems really started in high school. Every year I was attracted to a particular teacher, a woman teacher, and I mean really attracted. At the time I wouldn't have admitted it. I was either unaware or ignoring that there was anything sexual behind it. I never let myself know about it until I was a couple of years older.

But I really went all out for these teachers. When I was having a class with my favourite one I'd get specially dressed that day. I'd pay more attention to the way I looked and feel a little more self-conscious. I'd go out of my way to run into her in the hall. I'd get there early and go to the lobby to watch her arrive. It freaked me out. I saw it as abnormal and not right. I don't know if I was so hard on myself because my parents had taught me to be so critical of myself, or because I secretly knew that there was something sexual happening.

I also remember wanting to get her attention. Maybe if I were straight now I wouldn't be going back to those kinds of events and saying that was the start of it. It's not rewriting history; but I believe that that kind of thing could have happened to any kid — especially the kind that couldn't get the attention he or she needed.

I start feeling really anxious about it, and realizing, "Hey, I'm not having these kinds of feelings towards male teachers. What does that mean?" Then there was a whole series of events. When I was in grade ten I started to get so concerned about the issue that I went to see a guidance counsellor and she freaked out when I described what was going on — how I was going about getting attention from the teachers and stuff. She said to me, and I still remember it, "I don't have any training in psychiatry or psychology so I don't feel that I can help you." I just thought, "Oh, no. Something's really wrong. Maybe I'm crazy. Maybe I shouldn't be around." I was just getting more depressed, and more anxious and more closed off. It got really blown up.

She recommended that I go to see a doctor. So I made an appointment with one. Not my family doctor because I was too paranoid for that, but a doctor in the city who was of my parents' religious persuasion, because I figured that he would understand. That was a big mistake. What he did with my story was to say, "Well, have you ever heard of the word lesbian?" I said, "No," because I wasn't entirely sure what it meant, and he said, "Do you know what homosexuality is?" And I said, "Yes." And he said, "That's what you've got. If you ever need to talk again make another appointment." He was the doctor. He diagnosed it.

I just felt like taking a long walk off a short pier. I'm consigned to a life of weirdness. I didn't talk to that many people, and the opinion of people in authoritative positions really meant a lot to me, so I really took it to heart. And then to my great embarrassment my parents got a bill in the mail from the doctor and asked me if I was pregnant. I blushed at the mention of it, because I'd never even done anything with a guy.

My mother phoned the guidance counsellor who told her that I was really self-conscious that I had small breasts. I had also gone to see her about that. Mother told me that I shouldn't be embarrassed and there was nothing wrong with me.

In a sense when I try to think back to details of those years I think I block quite a lot because I would just rather not remember.

I know that I got very depressed, that I felt suicidal, although I never made any attempts. I thought, "I'm never going to amount to anything. I'll never be happy. There's no hope for me." I went through periods of really feeling quite hopeless. I spent a lot of time being depressed and withdrawn. I also got involved with girls from church and I started doing other numbers like teaching Sunday school. It was expected of me because I was a good religious girl.

After high school I left home to go into psychiatric nursing. Now I had all this potential freedom and everyone in the church was praying for my soul. The temptation was there and I drank a bit like everyone else. I had a lot of conflict because my parents would disapprove so strongly. My father's parting words – and this is one of the few times he ever talked to me – were, "Oh, you'll go crazy yourself."

Now I don't really blame my parents. I guess they loved me and cared about me; they just didn't know how to show it. And my mother didn't know how to stop my father.

Anyway, somehow I managed to temporarily forget about the whole gay thing. I began dating a few different guys. I got into a long relationship with a guy I ended up living with. And we were involved for four years.

I still feel attracted to men, but basically in the last few years I've been involved in lesbian relationships. That's where I'm at right now.

It's hard for me to imagine now how I made it through those times because I was so bloody isolated from the meaningful contact that a kid needs. Also I have a really stubborn streak in me and that stubbornness has a positive side to it – I would survive. The fighting side won out. And I was getting some strokes, some recognition to get me by. One teacher and some of the religious people I knew like me and cared about me. They gave me more recognition than my parents. If I hadn't had that little bit of encouragement from others and the instinct to fight, I don't think I'd be around today.

Adolescence is the time when a young person attempts to define himself and to assert himself as an adult-to-be. He may have been shaped by many forces – his family, school, and friends – but ultimately he himself is responsible for colouring that shape, for putting his distinctive mark upon it.

An increasing number of young people are choosing to colour themselves gay. Sexual identity is a crucial aspect in the total phenomenon of self-definition. In our society males are supposed to grow up to have sexual relations with females, and females are supposed to grow up to have sexual relations with males. To have sex with a member of the same sex is to be labelled homosexual. Not only are labels bad, as we have already seen, but homosexuality is a bad label.

Despite a generally prevailing permissiveness towards other

94

people's sexual habits, and the effort of Gay Liberation to promote the message that gay is normal and acceptable, most people view it as an aberration which is to be at best tolerated, but certainly not emulated.

Our abhorrence of homosexuality is deeply rooted. The Judeo-Christian tradition expressly forbids it and views it as a sin. Both Old and New Testaments contain numerous references to homosexuality as a serious offence worthy of severe punishment:

> Even the men of Sodom, compassed the house round... And they called unto Lot, and said unto him, Where are the men which came in to thee this night? Bring them out unto us, that we may know them... Then the Lord rained upon Sodom and upon Gomorrah brimstone and fire from the Lord out of Heaven.
> Genesis 19:4,5,24

> Know ye not that the unrighteous shall not inherit the kingdom of God? Be not deceived: neither fornicators, nor idolators, nor adulterers, nor effeminate, nor abusers of themselves with mankind.
> I Corinthians 6:9

In fact, until 1968-69 homosexuality was a criminal offence in Canada, and in the United States it is still considered criminal in most states. Anita Bryant's successful crusade to legalize discrimination against homosexuals in the area of equal employment clearly showed the animosity towards the gay community. True, many people spoke out in favour of the gays, but Bryant and her supporters won because they touched on very emotional issues. They appealed to people's fear and ignorance about homosexuals by saying things like, "Gays are pedophiles. We don't want them teaching in the schools and corrupting our children." No parent wants a homosexual son or daughter.

Homosexuality is thus undesirable, feared, and forbidden, but it is a terrible dilemma for the young person who finds himself in it. Not only does he feel guilt and shame because he thinks he is what he's not supposed to be, but he also feels he is a failure, because he "failed" to fulfil something as simple and as basic as his (or her) sexual role. One young man said, "By the time I was fifteen I knew there was something wrong with me. I would watch wrestling matches and have spontaneous orgasms. I had no interest in girls at all. But I couldn't let on because I didn't want to hurt my parents, and I couldn't face other people laughing at me. I felt so worthless! And such a hypocrite! By the time I was nineteen I was heavily into drugs, to the point where I was spaced out most of the time. I was deliberately trying to destroy myself."

Laura Z. Hobson has written a remarkable book called *Consenting Adult*, about how a family changes and develops because of a homosexual son in its midst. She recounts how the boy reacts to his first gay encounter. He is terrified that he'll be found out. He's always on the lookout for the car his sex partner was driving; he feels hunted. So the guys at the boarding school he attends won't suspect anything, he fabricates stories about his success with the girls back home. He fears he can never be like the guys, but he can't acknowledge his difference. He's tortured and ridden with self-hate!

And yet, it's not unusual for any person with any degree of introspection to wonder if he has homosexual inclinations, in the same way that most people have thought of suicide at one time or another.

The reaction to both is fear – fear of succumbing. Perhaps homosexuals arouse such antipathy in straight people because the straights fear that they may be contaminated, that they too have it in them to become gay. That would go a long way to explain the aversion many men have to ballet, and male ballet dancers in particular. They see them dancing in leotards with their genitals accentuated, their bodies making graceful gestures, and they immediately classify them as "fags." If the men are repulsed, it is only because they've been trying to repel their own worst fears.

According to one study published in 1973, five per cent of thirteen to fifteen year old males in the US have had one of more homosexual experiences, as compared with six per cent of girls in the same age group. For boys sixteen to nineteen years old the figure rises to seventeen per cent. The figure for girls at that age remains at six per cent.[2] So a homosexual encounter is hardly an unusual experience for a teenager. But there is a vast difference between the curiosity and experimentation of a few homosexual encounters, and homosexuality as a predilection and lifestyle. The adolescent involved, however, may not be able to distinguish between the two, partly because of his inexperience, and partly because he is trapped by the labelling process. "Thus a person comes to identify himself as homosexual. The social stereotyping is bought and becomes a personal stereotyping. Personal identity is tied to the label. The social role of deviant becomes the only viable avenue to attaining and maintaining an identity . . . they confuse the worth of a person with that of a characteristic."[3]

The poor self-image that is the result of this kind of labelling can lead quite easily to depression, isolation, and withdrawal. Convinced that he is worthless and will be so forever, a person may ultimately look upon suicide as the only solution.

If the problem of homosexuality is complex for the adolescent, it is no easy one for the psychiatrists and other social scientists who try to grapple with it. The confusion can be seen in the attempt just to find its cause. The most respected authority of all, Freud, assumed that:

Every person is constitutionally bisexual, which means that he inherits the tendencies of the opposite sex as well as those of his own sex. If the feminine tendencies of the boy are relatively strong he will tend to identify with his mother . . . if the masculine tendencies are stronger, identification with the father will be emphasized. . . . It is the relative strength and success of these identifications which determine the fate of the boy's character and his attachments, antagonisms, and the degree of masculinity and femininity in later life.[4]

Freud never considered homosexuality an illness. In a letter to the mother of an American homosexual who had written to enlist his help, Freud wrote, "Homosexuality is assuredly no advantage, but it is nothing to be ashamed of, no vice, no degradation, it cannot be classified as an illness: we consider it to be a variation of the sexual functions produced by a certain arrest of sexual development."[5]

Other researchers regard it as a destructive illness which has reached epidemic proportions and which is caused by social disturbances. "Affluence, proximity, leisure, the lack of definition of the two sexes, and changing functions ... in child-rearing may be creating a homosexual society."[6] Some see it as being caused by poor family situations, where the one parent is overbearing and the other weak, causing identification problems.[7] Others are more tolerant and approach "homosexual and heterosexual behaviour [as] merely different areas on a broad spectrum of human sexual behaviour ... and neither can be assured to be intrinsically more or less 'natural' that the other."[8] Still others see it as being caused by insufficient hormone production.[9]

If experts have such difficulty in defining the problem, it is little wonder that inexperienced adolescents may have trouble coping with it. But whatever the causes, why do there seem to be so many young people practising it? The obvious answer is that because of a more permissive, or at least less primitive, attitude towards homosexuality in the last few years, more young people are prepared to experiment with it. One seventeen year old said, "I think everyone wonders what it might be like, you know, whether they would like it and what they would do. Well, I decided to find out. Both the guys were close friends of mine, and both were as curious as I about it. It wasn't as scary as I thought it would be, and it was fun; but it wasn't all that great either. I don't think I'll try it again now that I know, but who knows? But there have to be deeper reasons."[10]

For some women, the influence of the Women's Movement has a strong effect on their sexual behaviour. In many ways a lesbian relationship is the logical outcome of a movement which makes unacceptable some concepts of masculinity and femininity. If women can't turn to men because men will put them down, treat them as less than equals and force them to accept the traditional role of inferiority in the relationship, then they will turn to other women. Though this attitude may make political sense, it can create a great deal of confusion in the lives of the young women who attempt it.[11]

For some adolescents the acceptance of homosexuality as a lifestyle is a way of acting out, of flaunting social values, and of hurting the people they feel have hurt them most – their parents. In the process they hurt themselves most. One adolescent boy put it this way: "My analyst sees my homosexuality as a continuation of my belligerence. According to him I've tried suicide twice and that didn't work, so now I've got this new thing to keep everyone else away from me, but at the same time to draw attention to myself and to let them know I'm around. I don't know if he's right, but I will admit one thing: I really enjoyed telling my father I was gay. It was my way of saying, 'You've been a failure as a father and this is how I'm rewarding you.'"

There are many philosophers and social scientists who view homosexuality as an indication of decadence in our society.[12] Whether or not homosexuality is decadent is beside the point; what matters is that it exists. But we can't avoid looking at social changes as contributing to increased homosexuality, or at least, to overt displays of it. Most social scientists would agree that children learn to fulfil the sexual roles that they are intended to play by imitating their parents, who serve as role models.[13] [14] If a father or mother is absent from the child's life, how is he supposed to learn?

Social roles are changing and expanding. It's all right for women to drive tractors, carry guns and be corporate executives, and for men to be nurses, secretaries, and to nurture children in a fashion that was previously considered exclusively "motherly." These changes are for the better, to be sure, because they don't restrict people to the narrow confines of role-playing. But they are happening so quickly that they can be painfully confusing for adolescents who have to make choices. One fifteen-year-old girl expressed the dilemma. "Everyone keeps telling me that I'm smart enough to be a doctor or an engineer. My parents are really pushing me. But I don't want to do that. I want to get married, have babies, and stay home and take care of them. What's wrong with me if that's what I want to do? After all, isn't that why God made me female?"

Another area of possible confusion in sexual roles is in the style of dress. Although a return to more "masculine" and "feminine" fashions is beginning, unisex fashions are still in, and it's very often difficult to tell the boys from the girls. There may be nothing wrong with that in itself, but it's one more area in which sexual distinctiveness is obliterated. To developing children these distinctions are crucial.

In short, despite the social injunctions against it, homosexuality is made easy in our society, in much the same way that suicide is. As the stories of Bruce and Liz indicate, homosexuality and suicide are closely linked.

Bruce's story paints an in-depth portrait of depression. The point at which Bruce realizes that he is different is the point at which his depression begins. How frightening it must be to face that moment of truth and to say, "I'm not like everybody else. I like guys." That knowledge sets him apart from others; it isolates him. He has a healthy desire to break through that isolation and reach out for help; but his efforts are rebuffed, thereby enforcing his belief that he is peculiar, and intensifying his loneliness and depression.

To make matters worse, what Bruce sees in the gay community terrifies him and drives home the fact that to be gay is to be socially condemned. We must admire Bruce's courage in that he is prepared to acknowledge to himself early on that he is gay, despite his psychosomatic illnesses. They can only be an indication of how difficult the problem is to handle.

Bruce finds no positive role models in the gay community, no one who can say to him, "Look, I'm gay, but I'm a happy person and I lead a productive life." What he must have seen were the failures, the people he must have termed "losers." So he flees from what he fears he may become. Like Howard, he resolves to handle his difficulties alone.

The method that he chooses for coping is doomed to failure. He tries to assert his manhood in the traditional *macho* way, by proving to himself and to everyone else that he can make it with the girls. Even if he does succeed outwardly, inwardly he derives no satisfaction from playing a role he's not suited for. He knows he's living a lie, and he's driven deeper and deeper into his depression.

He reaches the stage where he can no longer fight against his problems, and he seeks release. He finds it in a pill-induced state of sleep-death. Clearly, Bruce's behaviour is suicidal, but he has a marvellous self-preservation mechanism that keeps him from taking all the pills at once. He doles them out one at a time, just at a rate effective enough to keep him in a stupor. He can escape reality through sleep without having to resort to the irrevocable finality of death. Many people who do make suicide attempts want only the peace that comes with sleep; they don't want death. Lenore has already shown us that.

Indeed Bruce's sleeps do save him for a while. But they don't remove the causes of his depression, which not only remain untouched but become more complex. He eventually acquires a male lover, but finds that he's poorly equipped to take on a serious relationship and to make a full confession of his sexuality – he hasn't told his parents. As if that weren't enough all events conspire to overwhelm him so that all he wants to do is lie down and die. He is well beyond the stage of escape through sleep. This time he doesn't want to wake up.

Bruce knows that his parents would help if he asked them to but with the situation as it is he is too far gone to think straight. Finally, his parents don't wait to be asked. They step in and assume control, which is what Bruce really wants them to do. We have a lot of respect for his parents and we're sympathetic to their anguish over their son. They are always supportive, loving and non-judgemental. They're always there when he needs them and are prepared to give of themselves. We know that they must suffer terribly in watching their son, and they are prepared to let their son go it alone because that's the way he wants it. That kind of letting go takes a great deal of love and trust. But they're prepared to suspend the letting go for a while when they see how desperately Bruce needs them.

There is nothing punitive about their attitude. Surely a reproachful attitude would have driven him to suicide. Instead he's discovered how comforting the family bosom can be. When he finally announces his love relationship to them, they are warmly accepting. At no time does Bruce give us any indication that his parents are influenced by stereotypes, their own inadequacies, or by what people think.

And yet he is surprisingly unfair to them. He accuses his family of overprotecting him by not allowing him to work until he's nineteen, but in the same breath he tells us that his parents paid too much attention to his older brother. He says he didn't tell his parents that he was gay because of "normal adolescent alienation." That explanation is too facile. He's hard on his parents because it's easier for him to acknowledge his homosexuality by blaming them a little. He doesn't tell them he's gay because he's ashamed to. There's no getting away from it: Bruce is not yet comfortable with himself coloured gay; yet he has no alternatives but to accept it, however difficult it may be.

It is the dissatisfaction with himself that prompts his bitterness towards the psychiatrists who treated him, or more appropriately, he feels, mistreated him. According to Bruce, none of them responded to his needs by giving him and his problems the critical attention they deserved. Instead they were influenced by their own stereotypes and fears. Psychiatrists are people, too. Bruce makes the understandable mistake of viewing them as gods. Could he be bitter because he expected to be cured and had to settle for learning how to cope?

No one should underestimate the pain of discovering that one is a homosexual; it's not a state that most people joyfully welcome – to escape from pain is a normal human response. But the wisdom to accept what one cannot change comes with age. What drove Bruce to lead a suicidal lifestyle was his inability to cope with the pain. That he now feels that he doesn't have to die because he's different shows that he's come of age.

Compared to Bruce, Liz has a tough time of it at home. Her father is cold and rejecting, verbally and physically abusive, yet at the same time emotionally demanding. Her mother is passive, martyred, and unsupportive. Liz and her brothers live in fear. It's hardly the homelife conducive to growing up well adjusted. To compound her adolescent problems, Liz fears that she is gay. But perhaps she is gay because of her background.

> Examination [of families of gay women] shows a remarkably consistent picture. Homosexual women describe both of their parents in negative ways – the fathers as neglecting, moody, disappointing, unloving, mean, selfish, and untrustworthy, and the mothers as preoccupied with their marital worries and fears to the point of reduced involvement with their daughters. Overt interparental strife and child parent hostility are prominent. The home situation is essentially a Women's Liberation parody; cruel husband, martyred mother, and angry children. Understandably, the daughter who views her parents' relationship in this way is disinclined to adopt the traditional female role when it comes to male-female sexual pairing.[15]

It is very tempting to accept this as the total explanation for Liz's homosexuality. But to reduce her to a theory is to reduce her humanity, her uniqueness, and we could easily fall into the trap of not looking at her as a person. It is, however, interesting to learn that there may be many gay women who have family backgrounds similar to hers.

What we have to be concerned with is that her home life shaped her. It was directly because of the messages she was getting from her parents that Liz felt that she didn't count as a person. She wanted so badly to belong and be accepted as one of the group, yet she knew it could never happen. The suffocating religious beliefs of her parents made that impossible, because her parents saw association with people outside the fold as potential contamination. But even without the religion problem, Liz could never have joined. She never felt that she was good enough, not only as a person but as a body.

The fact that she is concerned about her small breasts is not unusual. Many adolescents, in fact many adults, are worried about the way their bodies measure up, or fail to measure up. But the fact that she is as concerned as she is – after all, she goes to speak to her guidance teacher about it – may indicate that under the anxiety over her bosom lies a more profound problem.

Repeated studies have shown that the more emotionally disturbed an adolescent is, the less tolerant he is of his physical self... Many adolescents who find that they cannot accept themselves for a variety of emotional reasons will project concern over themselves to some aspect of their appearance ... The child's assessment of his body reflects the values of those who take care of him. Children who are accepted by their families usually neither overvalue nor undervalue their bodies.[16]

Liz has singled out one aspect of her appearance through which she will label herself inferior. "I have small breasts. Therefore I am a worthless person." Also as Greta's therapist has already explained, one of the ways that a girl grows to feel good about being a woman is by the positive attention she gets from her father. But Liz's father gives her hostile messages, or at best ignores her; her mother makes her feel anything but good about her body – as we see when she had to explain menstruation – it's little wonder that Liz has negative feelings about her body, and by extension, about herself.

Liz develops into a shy, lonely, and depressed teenager, cut off from others. Like so many we have already seen, Liz too reaches out for love. She looks to her female teachers for love and encouragement. There is nothing in the least bit bizarre about an adolescent girl having an affectionate, admiring attitude towards an older woman. Good teachers can easily serve as models for their students. The fact that she takes extra care with her appearance isn't peculiar either; she wants to be noticed and approved of by someone she admires. As Liz herself says, "That kind of thing could have happened to any kid." But she feels that something must be wrong with her if she's behaving *that way*.

Her instincts are good in that she seeks help for her anxious feelings, but her encounters with her guidance teacher and her doctor only serve to establish her worst fears. She *is* crazy; she's been diagnosed, horror of horrors, as a lesbian.

It's no wonder that she becomes deeply depressed, hopeless and suicidal. The conviction that one is crazy is a secret that must not be shared; but in the frantic attempt to keep it to oneself other things get blown up out of all proportion. Sadly, the conviction often has no valid basis, but its detrimental effects can be lethal. Because Liz has been labelled "lesbian," she feels she is doomed to a life of weirdness or perversion or whatever else she imagines to be the implications of lesbianism.

It could be argued that her being labelled gay actually helps her to become gay. We know that she is very unsure of herself and has not had the example of a good male-female relationship in her parents' home. Can it be that in a relationship with a male she may find herself inadequate – not because of her sexuality, but because of her personality – and may use the gay label as a pretext to cop out of the relationship? It would be another way of putting herself down, saying, "Of course I can't handle this, I'm gay." Compare Liz with Bruce: He wasn't able to have satisfactory relations with girls, and his attempts to do so depressed him and made him feel he was living a lie. Liz, on the other hand, is quite comfortable in heterosexual relationships – sexuality itself isn't her problem. It's more a problem of how she feels about herself.

Her hopelessness is brought about by the belief that she is crazy and perverse and will never amount to anything. That's an awesome load of guilt for any person to carry, let alone a young person who feels totally isolated and without allies.

Yet Liz makes no suicide attempts. In fact, reading her story we get the impression that she is not suicidal at all; at most we feel that she was very depressed, but that she got over it. When questioned about her prolonged periods where she had constant thoughts of suicide, she was unwilling to discuss it. As she says, it's a period of her life that she's trying to block from her mind. We can understand from that how painful the issue of sexual identity in adolescence must be, especially if the identity is going to make that person a "deviant." Like Bruce she'd almost choose to die, rather than to be different *in that way*.

She involves herself in her church, in part because it gives her an opportunity to function in an environment where she is likely to meet with approval, and in part because it gives her an opportunity to expiate her guilt about what she feels is her sexual destiny. In addition, her involvement in the church gives her purpose. Liz also makes plans to leave home to become a psychiatric nurse. It's the ticket to freedom from her parents which she desperately needs.

Despite her hopelessness that nothing good will ever come of her, Liz has the psychic energy to point herself in positive directions. No doubt she wants very much to believe that she will amount to something. Without knowing it, she creates "carrots" to hold out for herself in the hope that tomorrow will be better. Her thought processes may have been suicidal for a long period of time, but she had the support of some people in her church and one teacher. With their help she is able to gather strength. Like Bruce she learns that a better tomorrow can come only if she deals with her sexual identity today.

5

THE BOY NEXT DOOR

Finally he could no longer hide and contain himself. His suffering became too great, and you know that as soon as suffering becomes acute enough one goes forward... Despair is the result of each earnest attempt to go through life with virtue, justice and understanding and to fulfil their requirements.
Herman Hesse, Journey to the East

George Walker began to panic. The snow was deep and night was falling, but his son Peter was nowhere to be found. Except for the whipping wind there wasn't a sound. Suddenly, about a hundred yards ahead, George could make out a large object lying in the snow. As he trudged forward he spotted a blue ski jacket. "Thank God," he thought. "That must be Peter. I hope he's all right."

It *was* Peter lying in the snow. Beside him was a shotgun. The side of his face and head were blown away. Around him the snow was red with blood.

George Walker fell to his knees and crumpled over his dead son's body. "Oh, no, God, no. Not my boy. Why? Why?" He caught sight of a patch of white protruding from the pocket of the blue ski jacket. It was a small index card on which a note had been scrawled in pencil. It read, "I have fought hard and the internal fight I had was hell. Look under my bed for the whole story. There are two packets underneath my bed. My love to all my friends. Love and peace, Peter. P.S. Sorry. Pity Mr. Chapman."

Four days later a memorial service was held for Peter. His teachers read the following tribute:

Today, with sorrow, regret, but still with solemn pride, Hillside Secondary School remembers Peter Walker, honour student, classmate and friend. Trustworthy and dedicated, Peter was a superior all-round student. Academically brilliant, he had maintained an average of 85% throughout high school. Intensely literary, Peter had read all Shakespeare's plays by the time he reached grade eleven. His reading library included lots of works of Nietzsche, Rousseau, and Voltaire. He was deeply concerned with and was unusually well informed on world problems. A good athlete, Peter participated well in competitive sports and was a good outdoorsman. Friendly, cheerful, positive, and conscientious, Peter was laden with an intellect and vision of life far beyond his age. Sensitive and introspective, he accepted the responsibility of the human conscience.

We cherish the memory of the loved, the respected, and the lost Peter Walker, who laid so costly a sacrifice upon the altar of peace and love.

Peter Walker lived with his mother and father and two teenage sisters in a rambling frame house in a small town. His father is a minister in the church. His mother is a schoolteacher who is actively involved in all areas of church, home, and school.

The older Walkers don't take their Christian commitment lightly. They practise it, opening their home to Indian kids in the area who need love and guidance and a roof over their heads: there was always four or five of them living in the Walker house. But the Walkers aren't the kind of people who go around preaching and converting. They just give of themselves with concern, with kindness, and with no strings attached.

The Walkers owned a private unspoiled campsite not too far from where they lived. The camp had to be made ready for spring. On a Thursday evening in early March Peter and his father set off for camp by train. The next morning they hacked ice for a few hours, then broke for lunch. After lunch Peter wanted to take a walk in the snow while his father napped. When his father awoke, he went out looking for Peter because there was still more work to be done before dark. He found him, dead in the snow.

Everyone who heard was shocked that this bright, cheerful person, who came from such a caring family and whose life held such promise, would kill himself. No one ever suspected that there was anything wrong with him. He just didn't seem like the kind of kid who would do such a thing. There was no motive they could find for insight or comfort. On the surface there was nothing unusual about Peter. He was the boy next door.

If everyone wanted to know why, Peter wanted to tell them. Those two packets hidden under his bed contained what he felt was the explanation for his suicide. In them were two crammed notebooks that contained poetry, a short story, and day-to-day reflections faithfully recorded in the year prior to his suicide. He wanted his writings to be read. That was his legacy to the world. Nothing else remains.

Excerpts from the Journal of Peter Walker

Apr. 14

Hello everyone. My name is Peter Walker. I'm presently fifteen years old, and I'm dead. Yes, dead. I'm trying to figure out how long I've been dead. I think now it's been about six or seven years. Actually, if you looked at me you wouldn't notice anything strange about me. I certainly wouldn't look like a dead person. But I'm convinced that I'm dead. I'm sure that

I'm not alive, so I'm either in a state of unbalance or I'm dead.
One thing for sure. I am not alive.

When I said I was dead what I really meant was that I don't
know what I am, where I am, now and going, what I'm doing
here, and in other words, I don't know anything. I'm just one
crazy mixed up kid who hasn't got the foggiest idea of what is
going on. I don't understand life, love, anything. I just keep
asking questions and getting nothing for answers. And it's
driving me crazy. I'm not content to live when I don't know
what it is to live. I must know all the answers. I will not be
satisfied until I know all the answers.

The Ladder

I am walking up a ladder which is my
Existence in time. The going is painfully slow
And I cry very often. My body cries and
My heart cries. There is no light to lead me.
And I have no destination, no motion
To keep me going. I can find no purpose.
I don't know why I'm alive. And if I were
To fall off this ladder in the deep dark depth
Below, why most people would start climbing
Again. But I don't think I would. And no one
Would care. And no one would even know that
I'm not there anymore. Because
　　　I
　　　　never
　　　　　really
　　　　　　existed.

I don't even know who I am. Something must have created me. But who and why? I am really an agnostic in this area. I say there must have been a creator or supreme being, but then again, did there really have to be one? And I think a creator of something would have control over what he has created. God is supposed to be so kind and right. But what kind of creator would allow such things he has created to kill each other and be so cruel to each other? The situation on earth has gotten out of control and I want to get off.

Right now I'm getting high on the Beatles, the greatest rock group ever to exist. I cannot really express my feelings for the Beatles. Things got so bad, that if I had not discovered them, I would have gone crazy before now. But am I really crazy right now?

I remember that great night. I had taken my brother's Beatles album and had played it with the headphones on. I remember it was Lucy in the Sky with Diamonds that really got me going. It was unreal. An experience which I had never experienced before. My whole body was lifted off the floor. I felt like crying for joy. Oh, Lucy, come take me away. I was really freaked.

My dream? My dream is living in a surrealistic world like the one in Yellow Submarine. I would really like to live in a world like that. It really takes me away.

On Dec. 6 I was going to kill myself. I typed up two copies of my final statement to the world. I look back at the events now and I see how strange the situation was. One copy was for my friend, Jim, the other for my parents.

I think the one thing that for sure will kill me will be my hair. When my hair goes, my life will go. Can you ever imagine a fifteen-year-old kid who is losing his hair? It's stupid. What kind of punishment is that? Well I'm fifteen and I'm starting to lose my hair. As long as it stays in I'll not even consider killing myself, unless something else happens. The second, the split second that my hair loss is noticeable, I will kill myself. BALDNESS CAN KILL, BUT ONLY THOSE WHO WANT IT TO.

May 27

The biggest fear in most people's minds is death. But I have no fear whatsoever of death. I am looking forward to it as a great adventure.

I think that as a child the subject which I first had questions about was death. I remember my first question was "What happens after death?" I can recall that I said that it might be worth killing myself to find out. I have always had such a great curiosity about death and after. Strange.

June 1

Christianity really bugs me because the whole house is full of it and my Mom and Dad eat it and breathe it, and Sandra is so religious it bothers me. But I wish I would go one way or the other, because you are really on a tightrope as an agnostic. That is the way my whole life is for me. A tightrope act.

The Delicate Balance

My life is balancing precariously
Like one rock on another. Any little
Movement or breath of wind could send me crashing
To the black depths below where no one walks
Away alive. I don't know where I'd rather be:
Living every second in suspense and
Struggling to stay balanced, or in the dark depths
Of the jaws of death. So I'm not too worried
About what happens, but I know I won't
Stay balanced for long. I just can't live in such
A delicate position. I must go either
One way or the other. And no one will be
Too upset if I happen to tumble.
Everyone will say, "Oh, it's such a pity
He had to die like that." Well, folks,
I only did what I had to do.

June 8

I really think that it would not be too bad to return to childhood when I was still ignorant. Strange, eh? As a teenager I
am learned and intelligent, and now that I am more informed
about the world I want to die.

Life is just one big dilemma and I'm stuck in the middle of
the horns, crying for help. I mean, I'm supposed to be so
smart now, but I can't stand and will not be able to cope with
my present situation for long.

I'm so strange. I seem to be such a moody person. Some-times I'm high, like after a good Reach for the Top game, or after a session with the Beatles. Then everything seems to go right. But other times I get so low that I could do a somersault under a worm. But strangely enough, every time I feel low, I always seem to enjoy living in a depression. I seem to like feeling really down. I think it's strange, but it's true. It's easy to feel bad and then retreat and lock yourself in a shell and then feel better. I think I'm always in my shell, but it's a shell of ignorance and mortality. I think and hope I can break the shell when I die. A shrink reading this after will say, "Aha. Here's a kid who was so reclusive he had to kill himself to be free." Well hold on to your pants, boys. You guys will never really know the whole story, so take it easy. I can never tell the whole complete tale.

To Marilyn K.

I'm sitting in the dark, there is no light
Sitting in darkness in a box which
I am locked inside and there is nothing
Inside this box. I stumble in the dark
And I search for something which I can't find
And there is no way out of this box. And I
Search and search and search and I don't even know
What I'm looking for, and I'll probably die
In that nothing box, searching for nothing.

I've had one of the most enjoyable times ever. Our chemistry class, about twenty of us, went out to a wilderness area to study a lake. We went out there for about four days. We had so much fun. I wonder why I can't enjoy life like I did this weekend.

The last night was the best. I could not sleep, so I got out of bed to talk to a couple of girls I knew in the nearby section of the cabin. I knew they didn't have a flashlight, and I thought it was dark enough so I didn't put on my pants. I only had on my underpants and T-shirt. I walked in and Ginny and Martha started laughing and giggling at me. My white underwear was very noticeable in the dark. Anyway, I sat on the edge of Ginny's bed and we talked. Then Barbara came in. I dove for the floor and hit my head on the wall. Ginny covered me up with her sleeping bag. Martha was laughing until she cried. I also couldn't help myself. Luckily, none of the boys woke up. I sat back on Ginny's bed and continued to talk to the three of them for about fifteen minutes. Then Ginny said, "All I want to see is your little white bum. Get up and leave." She was getting tired so I got up and went to bed. It was quite hilarious. It was the most fun I have ever had. Nothing really happened, of course, but I enjoyed myself. Mom freaked out when I told her.

I keep remembering and wanting to go back to that night. It was so much fun. But the trip had its low points. I kept getting the impression I was bugging people, especially Ginny. So I tried to correct myself and I couldn't. Maybe it was her, not me, but maybe it wasn't. I keep saying things that give other people the impression I'm conceited and smart. But I really try not to give these impressions and I tried to explain that to Ginny, but maybe it didn't come out right because she didn't get what I was trying to say. Maybe I'll write her a poem. I feel so confused.

I wonder what people will feel when they read this. They will always feel, "He's nuts. He must be. Only crazy people kill themselves." Well maybe I am crazy, but maybe I'm not. Right now I don't really know. I'll probably never really know. Maybe the whole world is crazy and I'm the only sane one. I may be crying for help, but I know no one can help me. I must help myself. That's the only way I can get any better.

I want to make something perfectly clear to those who will shrug off the event by saying, "He must have been on drugs." I have never smoked pot or done any other drugs up to this time in history. I doubt that I ever will. Right now I am satisfied with trips on Beatles. When I am no longer satisfied maybe I will turn to pot. Everyone at school thinks I'm into drugs because I guess I know so much about them.

I really can't believe it, the change that has come over me. In one day things have changed so much. On Friday Arlene invited me to her house for an early dinner so we could go and watch the basketball game. She is such a beautiful person I really can't believe it. So we took in the game and she drove me home. It was really nice of her. We're going to go cross country skiing on Thursday. We went last year and she had a great time. The experience last night had a great effect on my thinking. I changed from a pessimist to a half-optimist, you might say. How could I be so blind. There's such a change it's amazing. It really won't affect my outcome, but at least I won't die blind.

I'm starting to get glimpses of the rough world out there and it scares me. I mean I live such a sheltered dream life right now and I'm having problems, so what will happen if I'm exposed to the real world? I have to admit I'm very immature in many ways.

I realized that I am positively not crazy the other day. I am just having thoughts any normal person would have, but I'm writing them down. I wrote a sonnet about death in English. I know that seems to be a recurring theme in my poems, but I guess that's just where I'm at.

Death, a Sonnet

Who will not mourn for me when I am dead
Or even shed one tear in memory
No sky of rain will weep in silent dread
When final breath is gone in ebony.
And yet no man of high and mighty rank
Is mourned for endless years on infinite
But shed one tear for me, and that
To thank the one whose life of death
Was poorly writ. Yet mourn not long for me,
Although my days on earth were few
For by my death will I solve the puzzle
Of the life-filled maze from which I shall emerge
To die. No fear exists as I prepare my way;
Anticipate to meet death, any day.

(written in January, 1977)

Well, the sonnet is a heavy, you must admit, but I think for once it's not totally pessimistic. I think the sonnet brings out some points which are noteworthy. My fear of being quickly forgotten for example. I often stop and think, "It's only a trick. A game. It's not really going to happen. I'm only joking myself. I can't commit suicide. What? Am I crazy?" And things like that. Because oftentimes it all seems worthwhile, life seems worth living. But other times death is worth dying to get away from life. Like when you look at all the evil that man has done to the world.

Why I act so immature sometimes I'll never know. It really bothers me. I know I say stupid things and I try to prevent this, and yet I still do it. Ego, damn you.

Feb. 6

You know things sometimes aren't that bad. I feel pretty good right now. I just remembered that I could apply for World Youth and go to another country and work. That would be fantastic. It would really be something to live for. Who knows? I may even make it through the night. I'll have to get more info on it.

One thing I know about Arlene: she's a beautiful, beautiful person. I would really like to have a meaningful relationship with her. I do right now, but it's not close enough. I don't know if I could ever have a good close relationship with her. I don't seem mature enough. Maybe I just need more self confidence.

i missed your touch upon my skin,
i missed your love and warmth within,
But most of all, whoever you are,
i missed you.

Well it doesn't appear that I will be able to go in the Canada World Youth. It's for people seventeen to twenty and I'm only sixteen. It's really too bad, because if I could go in it I might have stuck to life as I would have had something interesting to do, something that I really wanted to do. But now I might as well go ahead as planned.

Feb. 10

I want my ashes spread out at camp. In the gardens at camp and in the stream. Let me be a part of what I am. Throw me in the soil where plants and flowers will feed off me and I will be a part of them. I will sprout each year and live forever. Reunite my ashes with Mother Earth. Don't stick me in some cage or in some box where it will take years for me to live as one with the earth. Please cremate me, it is my wish. But first, if possible, take my vital organs, if it can be arranged. I won't be needing them. There may not be much left of me, however. When will I see you again? Why have you forsaken me?

the last entry

Two things I really want to clear up. Some people probably think I'm a fag, but that's just because I don't flaunt my masculinity as others do. Also, some think I'm a miser. Actually, I just don't have any use for money, so I don't use it.

Where do I begin. The Beatles, Bob Dylan, Neil Young. Find the cost of freedom, lay your body down. Soul, weep. Mother Earth will swallow you. Bury near the ground. Life, I will miss you.

Peace and love,

Peter Walker

The Deathland

In the year two times two times two times ten
The animal man will breathe his last breath
And part his last parting. He will no more
Live to die again. For his own child,
That mushrooming red cloud of hate, has grown
To rule over the creator man; when unleashed
Strikes and annihilates with blinding fury
Leaving no babes spared. Its huge fire chokes
All, flattening the earth in its ghastly grave;
Spreading man's hate, turning all mankind
To black dust, dust, what remains of our life,
Dust. The wind shivers silently over the
Dead land, shaking its sad head as it whips
Unopposed over the lifeless planet. The earth
Will be as of the moon, silent, gray, ugly
Desolate, horrible, deserted, dead, gloomy. A
Torrid mass of rubble. Stony, wretched rubble.
No water, dust. No trees, dust. No Beatles, dust.
No life. Dust. Blackness will fall. The light of
Life will be extinguished forever. Look out,
Cause here she comes, she's coming down fast
Ostrinfin, objejuick, obajed . . .

The Story of Retep Reklaw

Retep Reklaw was in constant search of peace and freedom. Freedom from his problems, freedom from his sisters and parents, freedom from the whole world. He wanted a solution, a relaxant, to make him forget all of life's problems. As the days passed Retep found life more and more tense and increased his search for serenity. Retep found part of his solution at school. He was in grade ten in the local high school and faring well. And to make things even better there were many pretty girls at school. But Retep found problems at school. He was not athletically developed. His skill and coordination in many sports was lacking. Retep found himself being heckled constantly by classmates.

Retep worked hard to get his good marks and therefore was often very tired after a day of schoolwork. He searched for a badly needed means of relaxation but his search was in vain. Therefore he found some pleasures but more problems at school.

Retep stepped off the bus and headed home. The week had been a terrible one and the effects were showing on Retep. Retep had made an error of judgement in the volleyball game which had cost his team the victory. His teammates threw insult after insult at him. He felt relieved to get away from that group of "friends." Retep had received during the week four hard tests as the mid-term report card was coming up. Retep was worried about the results of the tests. Arriving home, he was confronted with a note telling him to shovel off the walk. He cursed, but finished it in fifteen minutes. As he stepped in the door his mother confronted him again. "Don't take off your coat. Here's a list of things I need from the store. I forgot to go this morning when I had the car." "It must be twenty below outside. I'm not going to freeze my behind because of your mistake. You can go yourself."

"Now don't talk back to me, son. You do as you're told. On your way you can make an appointment with the barber. Your hair's a mess. It looks disgraceful."

She had ignited him to a point where his flame could not be

doused. He flew into a rage and, doing something he never would have done lest he hurt her, struck her with his fist. He stared at his hand for a moment as they both stood stone-faced. The room became silent and the air became dessicated as the intensity of the situation developed. He turned and fled upstairs to his room. He quickly locked the door and collapsed on the bed.

Resting for a few minutes, his mind was a kaleidoscope of a thousand thoughts. His mother screaming at him, his "friends" screaming at him, the whole world screaming at him. Retep dropped off to sleep. Waking half an hour later his head had stopped spinning. Everything was stark and silent. He sank back and observed his room. It was small, and its appearance seemed to make him feel safe, beckoning him to continue resting. Retep was now isolated from the outside world, that dirty world which he despised. He was safe from reality. Here was his answer.

Retep found a stick of incense and, lighting it, placed it in a cup. The sweet oriental smell then filled the room. He found his cassette recorder and shoved in a tape. The Beatles started singing. "He's a real nowhere man, sitting in his no-where land, making all his nowhere plans for nobody. Knows not where he's going to, isn't he a bit like you and me." Disgusting, he thought. Angrily he flipped the forward button wildly. He stopped it as he cooled down and set the machine on "play." The Beatles were still singing. He was about to change it when something made his hand stop. The music was strangely relaxing. "Let me take you down 'cause I'm going to strawberry fields." He started going off into a dream as the incense drifted about the room. His body was completely relaxed and his body floated above the bed. His glasses slid from his nose and dropped to the floor. He did not try to pick them up. Although he could not see anything, he found the darkness better without them. They were a symbol of that world, and he felt better without them. His mind was a total blank and he found it to be a pleasant feeling. "Nothing is real, and nothing to get hung about, strawberry fields forever."

Retep felt a sensation he had never experienced before. The music and incense filled his body, and for the first time Retep Reklaw was not at war with the world. "Living is easy with eyes closed, misunderstanding all you see." The music called him further in, as he lit one incense cone after another. When he lit them all he was more relaxed than ever. He was in his own world where he was king. "It's getting hard to be someone, but it should work out, it doesn't matter much to me."

Retep's mind became hazy and his thinking unclear. He was not afraid, however, because there was nothing to be afraid of. There was nothing but peace, beauty and tranquillity. And nothing to get hung up about. "Strawberry fields forever."

When the police broke the door down the music had stopped and the incense was no longer burning, but Retep Reklaw, lying on the bed, was finally at peace.

FAREWELL LETTER
(written over a year before his suicide)

Dec. 6, 1975

To everybody:

Please don't misinterpret what I have done. I want no one person to take the blame. It was my decision, and I am not sad that I did what I did. There are very many reasons why I did this. First, and this may seem strange, I am very curious as to what happens after death. Sorry, Mom, but I can't take what the Bible says as the Gospel Truth *(heh!)*. I really am an agnostic.

Secondly, everyone will die sooner or later by old age or an atomic war, so why not sooner.

Thirdly, the pressure of schoolwork and homework were just too much. With six big projects going at the same time I knew I just couldn't take it. And if it's this bad now it sure won't get any better in university.

Fourthly, sorry Mom and Dad, but you must admit we didn't have very good relationships. You drove me nuts sometimes, Mom, and I probably did the same to you.

Fifthly, I see the world turning into an evil place. There is too much corruption, exploitation, misery, and pain. If people say, "Oh, it's too bad he's dead, and I'm happy to be alive and living and well," then the situation might change. I am hopeful.

Sixthly, I am really screwed up in so many areas. I have so many questions about life and no answers. It really got to me. I think I really said this in my poems. My poems and my short story will tell you everything you want to know. The Beatles played the biggest part in my "life." They really helped to relax me. They really did more for me than anything else. Oh, how they would make my body and soul float in the air. And I always cried when I realized that they are no longer producing music together.

I believe that pure Marxism is the best possible society. No class distinction. Everybody at the same level. That's beautiful. So I guess I am like Joan and Craig and am dying for peace and love.

I thought having a religion was important. Mine was a mixture of Buddhism and Christianity, but I could not take all the stuff in the Bible about miracles, etc., which don't seem to be possible. Buddhism tries to eliminate the thought of "I." It appeals to me because it stresses the finding of truth within your own mind.

Dad, I thought you were an okay person. You really tried to get things right for the Indian. I hope you continue and that you are successful. You really amazed me in that you always had a joke for the situation. I think you may come up short this time. You treated me well and I thank you for what you have done for me.

Mother, I know you will rest most of the blame on yourself. Don't. It was my decision. We did argue a lot. I really didn't understand you and I know you didn't understand me. Although I bothered you a lot and vice versa, I realize that you have gone through a lot, and I thank you for the help that you have given me.

Arlene, you were a beautiful person and I hope you continue in that path. You were very close to me and I know this will affect you in many ways. I thought you would answer my poems and was very disappointed when you didn't. I really felt a love between us and it was nice. I loved you in many ways. You always amazed me with your strict belief in God. I will remember you and my mind will think of you often. Remember me. Love, Peter.

Jim, you were a very close friend and I enjoyed your companionship. Try to remember what I have taught you. Try to pick up where I left off. Above all, keep going and fight for betterment. Remember me, Peter.

I want to say thank you to all my teachers over the years. I'm sorry it did not work out better.

"Many times I've been alone and many times I've cried; anyway you'll never know the many ways I've tried." (Beatles)

"Living is easy with eyes closed, misunderstanding all you see. It's getting hard to be someone but it all works out. No one I think is in my tree. I mean it must be high or low." (Beatles)

"All the lonely people, where do they all come from? All the lonely people, where do they all belong?" (Beatles)

Please don't hassle my friends about this. They knew all right, but they sure tried to talk me out of it. My last request is to play *Strawberry Fields Forever*, and *A Day in the Life*, in that order, at my funeral. Please don't deny me that much. Keep trying for peace and love.

Peter Walker

If Peter's journal, poetry, and short story reveal beyond any doubt that he was depressed and suicidal, it came as a shocking surprise to all those close to him who read what he had written. His parents, his sisters Rita and Sandra, his closest friends Jim and Arlene, all said that the writings reflected a Peter they never knew, a sad, hopeless, confused, tortured, and desperately unhappy teenager. If the signs were there in his life, then they missed them. What follows are their accounts in their own words of how they viewed Peter.

Arlene

I first met Peter in grade nine. He was a really neat guy. He liked me. I was wearing a yellow dress. He liked my yellow dress and always wanted me to wear it. We became really close friends in grade nine.

He loved everybody. I can honestly say that. This love just shone out of him. You could feel it. He was never mean or cruel to anybody. He'd always laugh, and always try to help people. He'd give himself to anything, to anybody. And the gang that he was in at school, well, they were different from other guys. They weren't as cool. But these are the kind I like, that can relate to you.

He was different from other kids because he was tall and unco-ordinated, but he was really smart. Some of the kids really didn't take to him. But I'm the kind of person that if they're not exactly friends with everybody, I'll be their friend. That's the way I was with Peter. But I sort of tried to keep him away at the same time. I didn't want him to get emotionally attached to me. I was scared of that. I liked him as a friend, but that's as far as it could go. I didn't want to hurt him by telling him that I didn't like him.

There was never a physical relationship between us. Just once he asked if he could kiss me. I said no, because I couldn't. Then I remembered it was New Year's. I embarrassed him so much. I came over on New Year's Day and I said, "Well, where's my New Year's kiss?" and he just gulped and stammered and said, "Uh, no. I don't think so." And then I knew that if he wanted something really physical, he just couldn't give it either. He wrote in his journal that he wanted more out of our relationship but that he wasn't mature enough. He was very mature. It's just that I treasured him more as a friend than as a boyfriend. That's just the way it had to be.

Girls had never really taken to him as a guy. He was just the kind of person you don't get physically close to. It had to be emotional or just friendship. That's just the way he was.

That time we had supper and went to the basketball game together. It was so neat. We really enjoyed it. I talked to him all afternoon and finally convinced him to come over for supper. He really enjoyed it. He was really a fun guy to be with.

But most of our friendship was tied up in poetry. He wrote a lot of poems and he'd give them to me. I'd read them and tell him what I thought. We did a lot of talking. We'd study together at school. A couple of times we went cross-country skiing and canoeing. It was really neat to be with him because he's really fun. But it was mostly with the poems.

When I first met him I thought he was just a happy guy. But as I got his poems, I noticed that a lot of them had to do with death. It scared me. I didn't know how to react to it. I took it seriously. I was so scared that he'd try something. I went through two years just being petrified. I talked to him about it. Like his poem about the ladder, where he said if he fell off who would care? And I said, "Peter, I'd care." I got the impression that he didn't care about living, but he lived for the sake of everybody else. I don't think he ever thought of how much he'd hurt other people by dying.

He gave poetry to Marilyn K. too. We talked about it. She was the only one I talked to about it. I remember us being really scared. But when you're just living you tend to forget. And it's not good but it happens. I'm the kind of person that I get so tied up in life that I forget about death. And reading his poems, well I'd get one every six months, or something like that. I'd be reminded, we'd talk about it, and then that would be it for another six months.

I don't think the teachers took his stuff too seriously. I think they thought it was his imagination. The teachers at school tend more to give a mark and forget about it; they're not willing to become involved. And I know a lot of teachers were upset when he died, but I can't remember any of the English teachers being upset. They get so many essays and poetry, so many different messages that it just goes right through them. I can understand why they didn't understand.

The general reaction at school? A lot of kids at school just knew Peter superficially and they acted like he was their best friend. It just drove me up the wall. I was so close to him, I felt so close to him. When they read his poem over the PA system in school on Monday morning, I just broke down. I cried so much. I don't think the others really cared about him. It was just the shock of someone they knew killing himself. They'd never really had that happen to them before. I was so mad. I felt like just slapping them all.

He was having a lot of trouble finding where God was. And I believe in God. He'd come to me to ask questions. Last summer I was having trouble with God and that, and I wrote him and told him about it. He was just devastated. He thought I was such a strong believer. But I got over mine. He didn't.

He didn't accept a lot of stuff that the church taught us about God, about his love, goodness, and all. He couldn't accept it because he saw too much in the world that didn't seem like that. I don't think he really cared if God loved him. He didn't understand God. He wanted to figure him out and he wanted to do it on his own. He didn't really want anyone else including God to help him.

I don't think his situation at home helped him to figure things out. Whenever I came to his house I got the impression it was more like a boarding house. Cause there are a lot of kids living there off and on. I knew that his parents were loving but I never saw any kind of physical love between the kids and parents. I felt I could never live in a house like that. I'd have to reach out to something else. Peter reached out to other people. His parents are great though. They're really lovable people and I know he really loved them. He was really open with his Mom too.

Peter's father was in the church and he helped the Indian

people. Mrs. Walker, she was just everywhere. I felt that Peter just got lost in the shuffle somewhere.

When I first heard that he'd killed himself, I didn't believe it. He killed himself on a Friday, and I didn't find out the truth till Sunday. I can remember how hurt I was. I couldn't believe that he would do that to us. I felt it was a betrayal, but yet I had the feeling that it was coming because of his poems. I knew that it could happen so I wasn't surprised when it did. But I was hurt.

I didn't feel guilty. I had no regrets. Usually when somebody dies you say, "Oh, I should have done this or that," but I thought, "If Peter wanted to do it, then that's what he did." And there's no way you could stop him really. Peter was the kind of person you couldn't really stop. If he wanted to do something, he just did it.

Nobody blamed me, thank goodness. Mrs. Walker, after the memorial service I came over and she really laid the questions on thick. Did I know, why didn't I say something? It was just that I didn't understand. I believed him, but I didn't think he'd go that far. But I knew it could happen.

I doubt if anything could have prevented his death. He'd obviously been thinking about it for a long time. In grade ten he started writing the death poems. Before that he'd write about animals dying. I'd gotten the impression that he was just that kind of person that thought about death a lot. I couldn't quite understand him. He was so deep. His poems when he'd write them to me, I couldn't quite understand them, you know. But there was some kind of death there.

He must have had a lot of build-up in him. Things just got too tense and he just said, "That's it. I quit." He couldn't stand it anymore.

You'd think his desire for death would have gotten lost after a few months, but it didn't. I don't know if things would have gotten better if he had hung on. It's almost as if he had programmed himself to die.

I think the reason he killed himself is in his poems. He loved people a lot and he couldn't face seeing people hurt or anything, or starving, or dying. All he could see was beauty. That's all he wanted to see. But he thought that by killing himself people would see how much they're missing. But his logic was a little off.

I think he felt inadequate about solving the big problems of the world, that he alone, well, he couldn't do that much. An average person can't make a big dent on the world. Maybe he thought that by killing himself more people would know. If that was his reason I don't think he succeeded with most kids. I don't think he took into consideration human nature, that they'd think about it for a day and then just forget.

He wasn't crazy, not at all. I had a lot of faith in Peter. I loved him as a person and as a friend. Nobody could ever say to me that he's crazy. I just couldn't accept it.

His journals seem well planned. When I read his journals I got the impression that he was writing a big book, almost for show. I know that if I kept a diary I would never want anyone else to read it. He didn't sound crazy in his journals.

Was he really crying out for help? I think so, because when he got my letter about God and everything he told me that he was just the biggest fool in the world and that he was just wearing a mask; that he wasn't really happy. He said he wanted to talk to me. Nothing really came out of it because we never had time to talk. And that's bad. I think now that if I had talked to him something might have helped, though I think he would have killed himself eventually.

Rita

Peter's death was a real shock to me. I just couldn't see him killing himself. I didn't think he had that many problems. That's the first thing we thought of – how unlike Peter.

Peter and I were the closest. We were up at camp together once sleeping in the same cabin. He told me that he had had his first wet dream and it was about me. I didn't know what to say. My boyfriend told me not to feel ashamed or embarrassed about

130

it. That same time at camp Peter made brownies and put dope in them. It was a brownie mix with two packages. He used one and sealed the box back up. When Mom came to use it she said, "Look at this. They ripped us off. There's only one package in here." He was really laughing. But I remember how pleased he was that he fooled Mom.

Mom never had any trouble with Peter and Sandra. But Bob and I always did things to bug her so she had to listen to us. Maybe she didn't have to listen to them. They didn't make themselves heard.

He resented the presence of the Indian kids because she was paying more attention to them and not enough to him. And it was a rough year for Mom with those kids. Before, Peter liked the kids, you could talk to them, and he got along with them. But these ones, they were more interested in going out or getting drunk. Everything just kind of built up. The boys would always tease him because he was so smart.

One day he showed us all the story of Retep Reklaw. He told us it was his name spelled backwards. I said, what do you want to die for? He said I don't know, it's just a story. It was his inner thoughts. I know there's no point saying it now, but we could have listened more, we should have looked at it better, we should have heard things that weren't really there.

What made me upset was that some of his friends knew and didn't say anything. Of course we knew about his story and poetry, but they knew that he had actually tried it. I can remember when I was in high school one of my girlfriends told me that she was going to kill herself. She had brought razor blades and Valium to school that day. When she suddenly wasn't around I got really scared. I told some of the guys and they found her in the bush area behind the school. She was in the hospital for quite a while. She never told me if she was glad or sad that I told, but today she's really happily married and has a child. So I guess that's enough proof there that she wasn't mad or anything.

His friends couldn't have done much. They have no knowledge, they're just his peer group. But maybe that's where it should have started.

Why? Each person has to figure it out in his own head. I think *he made up his mind, and he was the type of guy who once he made up his mind he couldn't back down. I think that in itself would kill him. He couldn't live with himself if he didn't do it, because he'd be all disappointed in himself and he'd say "you're nothing but a coward and a loser and you can't do anything." He had it planned out. I think he was having second thoughts, that he really didn't want to do it. But he had it in his head and he just couldn't get it out. He had just committed himself to it, and had to go through with it.*

He did it in such a no-second-chance, irrevocable way because that's him. He knew there couldn't be a second chance.

I think, too, that death was an adventure to him.

The Walkers

We knew that our son was different. From the time he was a little boy he was always very bright, very perceptive, very sensitive about other people. When playing with other kids he would never hit. He would always shy away from any kind of physical confrontation.

He could do absolutely anything he wanted to do. There wasn't anything he couldn't figure out. Nothing was beyond his scope. He read constantly and was always very interested in everything that was going on around him. But sometimes he was difficult to get along with because he was so rigid. Once he made up his mind about something, there was no way that you could sway him. If he had an opinion he would stick to it no matter what.

He never wanted us to interfere in his plans for his course of study or his social life or anything. He was very proud of his independence and was strong willed. He was a Walker – strong and silent.

Peter would always get into political discussions with us. He really enjoyed them and he was trying very hard to figure things out. He was annoyed with us for having had four children; he felt that was too many. When he had to do an assignment for school on the world food shortage he really got into it. It affected him deeply.

He resented the fact that the Indian kids were living with us. He particularly complained about it in the last year of his life. They may have been getting some of the attention that he wanted; yet he formed close relationships with some of them.

His hair was a great concern of his. Nobody noticed it except him and he exaggerated it out of all proportion. We told him that it didn't show. We tried to be sympathetic and caring, but no matter, he felt it did show. The last week of his life he parted his hair in the centre and went to school with it that way, so that the thinness of his hair was highly noticeable. He wore it that way until someone finally commented on the fact that his hair was thinning. It seemed that he really wanted to draw attention to himself in that way and possibly torture himself. He was also very self-conscious about his body, because he grew so fast that he was awkward and gangly.

He showed us the poems dealing with death and the short story. We said, "Peter, why are you so morbid?" and left it at that. He seemed so normal in other respects we never thought to go into it. It really seemed inappropriate. Now, of course, we know we should have.

We always made our son know that he was wanted and we bragged about his achievements. The whole thing is incomprehensible as he had never given us cause to worry. We were also shocked at his using a .22, as he just didn't care for guns, in fact, he had bought his own hunting bow. But hindsight is always 20/ 20. He did spend a lot of time in his room writing, and listening to the Beatles. But, he still maintained contact with his friends.

The week before his suicide he seemed a little more jumpy than usual, a little more agitated. But even in retrospect we still can't see that that was anything to be alarmed about. He was still going to school. He ate. He slept. He did everything normally. The day before he shot himself he was out on the street playing hockey with his friends. In the journals we saw a side of Peter that we didn't know existed.

We just can't bear to think that he suffered so long then died alone. The heavy burden of anguish over his terrible secret of

133

what he was planning to do must have been the hell he wrote about in his note. We wonder how he was able to harden himself to our daily expressions of love and concern. He was so good, and he was so hard on himself.

We feel he was a near-genius and just learned things that he couldn't handle emotionally. He kept saying that the world was cruel, that there was so much wrong with it, so much ugliness, and all he wanted was beauty. Maybe he was immature, too, as well as being young and idealistic. He just couldn't fit in. He was overly sensitive. That's why he killed himself. He wasn't crazy.

Sandra

I saw a whole new Peter when I was reading the journal, a very deep person that I didn't even know existed, because I just saw him as my brother. We had a lot of nice times together.

I thought we got along really well, but then Peter always felt I was favoured and would get mad about it. I could show my emotions and he couldn't. I didn't know he had trouble with his school work. I always thought he could whip off an essay like that and do it really well, too. When he gave trouble with his school work as one of the reasons for wanting to kill himself I was really surprised. Teachers are supposed to be aware of what's happening. If he was so unhappy about school and was giving them death poetry, how could they have missed it?

I can't remember him being depressed at all. He listened to his records a lot with his earphones on. Everything seemed normal to me. I remember him laughing a lot. So do my friends.

I really don't know if he was well liked. He wasn't a part of any group at school, but he was liked by all my girlfriends. I think he was well liked but he didn't participate in a lot of things, so he was there but not really accepted.

But I don't think he knew the right way to act around girls. I think he got frustrated easily; but he really did like girls. I remember one time he tried so hard to get a date with a girl. He wouldn't let me stay in the room. I heard him dialing and dialing, but no results. But he never showed me that he was depressed or anything. He just laughed it off and said, "I'll go with Jim." But I could tell that he was hurt that no girl wanted to go with him.

I know he had a special feeling for Arlene. There was something special about her that he really liked. I think that was something to look forward to. To be able to be with her.

Kids didn't praise him enough and I think he really needed that. Little things really hurt him, like the time he missed the ball in the volleyball game that he wrote about in the story of Retep Reklaw. The other kids just got angry with him at the moment. It was no big deal. I know because I helped to referee that game. But he took it so seriously. Anyway, his missing the ball didn't cost them the game.

I don't know if my parents were clued in. With Dad, you can talk to him but he'll never tell you how he feels. And Mom, I don't think she listens enough. I think she hears what she wants to hear. She doesn't understand. It's hard to communicate when that happens. She states her opinion a lot. You can't really say anything. But I think she really does try awfully hard.

Dad doesn't try enough. Sometimes I think he thinks about the Indian people and their problems too much, and doesn't realize what's happening at home, things he should know about. But Dad and Peter seemed to share a lot. They'd watch sports together, and go out to camp. I think we're a weird family.

I don't think Peter was crazy. He could have been helped if we had known. There's some hope for everybody. We would have done everything we could to help him. I would have listened to him, I would have tried to help him out. But he never talked to me.

I think if he had hung on a while longer till he was more mature he would have made it. Adolescence is such a tough time; so many decisions, you don't know what career to choose. He might have been able to sort out his own thoughts without resorting to death.

Jim

I've known Peter since '67. We became friends right away. We became friends so quickly because there was no one else around. We played hockey, fished. Peter was intelligent, had good marks in school. He was a pretty good guy.

I knew he had thoughts of death. In December '75 he mentioned it one day. And then one night he called me over. He'd been sick that day. He said he tried to take some poison, but it didn't have any effect on him. I couldn't believe it at first, really. Then he seemed to cheer up. I just let it slide by, especially since he said that God probably didn't want him to die right then. I'm still not sure if I believed it. We had a lot of tests and projects at that time, so that might have influenced him.

After that he seemed okay. The odd time he showed me in the encyclopaedia what death or suicide was, or what Hitler or someone else thought of it; but after that, nothing. He was really interested in death and was more interested in it as he went along. I thought it was because he was different from others. He read a lot of books and he never really told me too much about them. I just thought it was another one of the subjects he was learning about.

I was never worried about it. After that first time he seemed to cheer up quite a bit. I didn't give it another thought. I figured he was just curious about life after death.

I guess he was so interested in finding out what happened after death, he just couldn't wait. He'd read so many books, quite heavy ones, too, I'd say. That's all he ever did was read. But it didn't seem like something he'd do.

I know he was sensitive about his hair getting thin, but he was the only one who noticed it. Even when he told me I couldn't notice.

As far as I know he only had one date, if you can call it that. After a hockey game he asked a girl if she was going to the same pizza house as the rest of us. That's it.

If he was really depressed and thought the world so bad, he didn't show it, really. The night before his death he was out playing hockey with me and another guy. We all had a great time. I don't know what was depressing him really. Did he say?

From the first time he tried to kill himself until he did it, he must have spent that year making up his mind and deciding to go through with it. For sure, no second chances.

I still ask myself if there were signs I should have noticed. Maybe there was one. You know, the night before he died when we were out playing hockey, well I came back to his house with him, and he didn't look at me when I was talking to him. He was kind of looking away. That could have been a sign, but I didn't notice it right then. It could be that he was really saying goodbye to me in his way.

If I had known – I don't know what I could have done, really. I could have talked him out of it, or gotten someone else to talk him out of it. But he didn't show any signs, or not to me.

I found out from our minister. He came over and told me. I didn't believe it at first. In fact I still don't believe it. It seems like he's just gone away for a while and he'll be back someday. When the minister told us I came over to the Walkers. My dad came, too. We stayed a while and then went home again.

The reaction of the school was quiet. Especially on our floor where the lockers were. Not the usual noise. The whole school was pretty quiet on that day.

When I think about him, sometimes I think he was stupid. I think that if he could come back and look at it again he'd change his mind. He was curious about what happens after death, now he knows.

I got the letter after his death. I don't know if it really explained how he felt. His suicide was really stupid. If he really cared so much about the world he would have stuck around to help straighten it out. He left a lot of big jobs undone.

Peter's story is astonishing because of the obvious similarity it bears to Howard's. It has a somewhat unsettling effect on us because we could cope with Howard's story by classifying it as a case unto itself. Now along comes Peter with a carbon-copy tale. Is the world full of Peters and Howards, or was it just sheer chance that in the course of research I happened to stumble upon two similar people in similar situations? Perhaps both. As fascinating as the comparison with Howard may be, we should remember that it's only the arbitrariness of this book that has thrown them together. But there may be something to be learned from the way they responded to their common problems, so comparing them is inevitable.

Anyone familiar with the well-known journals of teenagers, *Go Ask Alice* and *The Diary of Anne Frank*, knows that they were intensely private documents. Both girls were recording their innermost thoughts and feelings so that they could unburden themselves of their problems and in this way, perhaps, master them. The journals were silent but devoted and ever-present friends whose chief function was to listen. Indeed, the anonymous author of *Alice* personifies her journal and refers to "her" as "Dear Diary." Anne Frank calls her journal "Kitty." In both instances a very intimate relationship developed between the girl and her "friend." Everything was revealed. Nothing was censored as being unsuitable for public consumption, because there was no public intended. The fact that both journals have survived for posterity is purely a matter of circumstance. Neither of the girls expressly wished it.

Peter's journal is markedly different. From the very beginning we become aware that he is addressing himself to a large audience. "Hello everyone. My name is Peter Walker. I'm presently fifteen years old and I'm dead. Yes, dead." He immediately wants to shock his audience into paying attention to him. And if we didn't see it the first time, he repeats his startling piece of information so that we are certain to know that he's dead. He doesn't want us to ignore that fact.

His writing is very self-conscious and he is constantly aware of being judged by his readers. Consequently, he's defensive. Peter doesn't want his journal to be an intimate, soul-searching confession, and he says so explicitly. "You guys will never know the whole story."

So this is no ordinary journal. It's a public document wherein the writer presents the same problems over and over again, without much insight, and without total sincerity. His whole journal is one long lament about how rough life is for him. He wallows in self-pity. As a result, we may find his journal unengaging, and we don't have much respect for Peter because he won't even attempt a good fight. He is already defeated.

As readers, Peter's journal places us in an uncomfortable dilemma. On the one hand, we feel morally bound to like him and to believe everything that he tells us because he died for it, and because he specifically mentioned in his suicide note that his writings would provide the explanation. On the other hand, he has destroyed some of his credibility by addressing us so readily, by his constant complaining, and by telling us that he is deliberately going to withhold information from us.

How do we proceed? We can't in good conscience shrug off his journal as insincere ramblings, because that's not true either. We do get the gut feeling from reading the journal, poetry, and short story that this kid really hurts and is desperately trying to tell us why and how it feels. We also have Howard's remarkably lucid account of why he kept a journal, which makes us more receptive to Peter's. His plight is legitimized. We cannot view him as insincere and a player of games. But at the same time we have to try and leave ourselves open to answers that might come from areas outside his writings, mainly the accounts of those who knew him, and our own feelings.

The composite picture that we get of Peter Walker reveals to us a young person becoming aware of the contradictions of life: beauty and ugliness; good and evil; wealth and poverty; truth and lies. At the same time he is himself full of contradictions. While he is so concerned with major world problems, he is also extremely self-centred. He is very righteous about being honest and truthful, yet he sometimes distorts the truth. (He denies ever having anything to do with pot, while his sister Rita expressly tells us that he has.) He strives so hard to be independent, yet it's painfully apparent that he needs people. He wants so badly to succeed in life, yet he's determined to self-destruct.

Except for his glaring preoccupation with death, Peter is

much like any other adolescent. He loves/hates his parents, school sometimes gets him down, he has a favourite rock group, and he's frantically concerned with his appearance. To be accepted and liked by his peers, especially girls, is vitally important to him, and his skill in sports is part of that. He wants very badly to fit in. He also wants answers to crucial questions such as God, love, and the purpose of live, and he wants them *now*. He's eager to make a meaningful contribution to the world, and he wants to do that now, too. His thoughts of death and the knowledge that he has the power to take his own life are not unusual – only the extent to which he dwells upon them. And he has mood swings – sometimes up and sometimes down.

But what is it that makes Peter so concerned with death? He tells us that he's been curious about life after death since childhood. We know that he has read a lot about it. But his interest is more than academic. He is involved; he is deeply committed; death becomes his passion on which he will lavish his emotions and energy. He tries to free himself from its suffocating embrace, but he is never successful. Death has such strong appeal because it represents the ultimate escape; and he's always on the lookout for escapes because he can't cope with life.

One of Peter's big problems is coming to terms with God, the Christian version in particular. It's an especially troublesome issue for him, since he has obviously been strongly reared on Christianity. We can understand his questioning and attempted rejection of Christianity. His father is a minister and "the whole house is full of it." Peter is not the kind of person who accepts ideas readily unless he has tested them himself, so he certainly isn't going to accept his parents' religion without rigorous scrutiny. Yet he can't handle the consequences. If God exists and God is love, why is there so much cruelty and hatred in the world? "The situation on earth has gotten out of control and I want to get off." He immediately seeks his escape route.

His wanting to know the big answers to all the big questions immediately is hardly unusual. We've encountered this before in Huck Finn, in Holden Caulfield, and perhaps in ourselves. But Peter's approach is inherently destructive and designed to fail. He's got to figure it all out on his own because to get help would be an admission of failure. He views himself as a strong independent person; he feels he's expected to behave this way because he's a Walker and he's "supposed to be so smart." The tragedy is that he actually conceives of it as a weakness to have to share his problems with someone else. He does make attempts through his writings, but no one takes him seriously because he's supposed to be so smart and so independent. That's how everyone sees him.

Not surprisingly, this dilemma is driving him crazy, as he admits; and it is this feeling that isolates him even further. The rationale goes something like this: "I am unhappy. I have thoughts of death. I must be crazy. Normal people don't have thoughts of death. So I'd better keep it to myself and not let on to others, because if they find out, they'll think I'm crazy too." He deals with his problem in characteristic fashion. He withdraws into his shell, as he aptly refers to it, and fantasizes about death.

We saw this in Howard too, but the advantage that Howard has over Peter is circumstance. His adolescence just happened to take place at the time of the Vietnam war. Sure his participation in it was a veiled suicide attempt, but it was also a pretext to stay alive. Here was not only a heady cause worth fighting for and providing some justification for his living, but it was also a channel into which he could direct his hostility. As we saw with Mark in Chapter Two, delinquency and suicide are two sides of a single coin. For Howard, his manner of participation in the anti-war movement also provided him with social acceptability. Sadly, there is no convenient *raison d'être* for Peter.

What he wants more than anything is to be accepted. The only entries in his journal where he is hopeful and exuberant have to do with the possibility of his being accepted by others, whether it is the girls in his chemistry class, Arlene, or World Youth. In all three instances he feels optimistic and is quite willing to put aside thoughts of his own death. But the girls really don't like him (including Arlene, despite all her protests to the contrary) or at least they don't like him in the way he so desperately wants to be liked, and he's too young for World Youth. He blames himself, and his hopes quite literally turn to ashes. He seeks refuge in death.

Peter is painfully sensitive, mostly about himself. We often get the impression that his concern with world problems is only an extension of the concern about his own personal problems. If all were right with him, then all would be right with the world. His missing the volleyball and being shouted at by his teammates in the heat of the moment is tantamount to a death sentence for him. He feels that he deserves to die. He reacts similarly to his thinning hair. His self-esteem is so low and his method of coping so poor that he would actually choose death over baldness. It's no accident that the week of his suicide he wore his hair parted in the centre to draw attention to the fact that it was thinning. He needed confirmation that he was unworthy and deserved to die to give him the courage to pull the trigger.

The various escape routes that Peter considers – childhood, sleep and the Beatles – soon merge into one. Death. He doesn't know what death is, but he fancifully imagines it to be like the worlds of *Lucy in the Sky with Diamonds, Yellow Submarine*, or *Strawberry Fields*. The Beatles strike all the right sympathetic chords within him. Not only do they conjure up fantasy worlds that appeal to him, but their songs provide a confirmation of his feelings by responding to his depression and the way he views himself. Like Howard he uses the lyrics of songs to enforce his distorted view of himself and the world. For both of them the lyrics assume an almost holy significance.

Anyone familiar with the Beatles' music would be hard pressed to agree that their music is as strongly suggestive of death as Peter thought it to be. But there was a lot going on in his troubled mind. He was trying to resolve all problems himself, without knowledge, without experience, and without mature judgement. He read into the Beatles what he wanted to read into them. They were adapted to suit his needs.

Peter did the same with Joan and Craig. In his "trial" suicide letter he mentions them, saying, "So I guess I am like Joan and Craig and am dying for peace and love." Who are they? None of Peter's family or friends knew, but they all suspected that there was an important link between them and Peter. Indeed, they were right.

Craig and Joan, by Eliot Asinof,[1] is the true story of two teenage lovers who killed themselves to protest the Vietnam war. On the surface there are many striking similarities between Craig and Peter, certainly similarities that Peter must have recognized and seized upon as justification and endorsement for taking his own life. Craig is described as never being "satisfied with half-hearted or less than genuine responses. He wanted everyone to be real and honest, and he discovered the best way to evoke these qualities in others was to communicate with a sense of love." Craig was very involved with folk music. His brother estimated that he spent forty hours a week with it. Not surprisingly, he rejected the values and aspirations that society had declared worthy of emulation. "What annoyed Craig was not the money they [society] had, but their total involvement with its pursuit, and always at the sacrifice of any meaningful involvement with other people. This, of course, was at the root of his interest in joining the Peace Corps." Peter too, would look to an equivalent of the Peace Corps as a possible solution to his problem.

We are also told that towards the end Craig was content to stay in his room alone a lot, writing poems, stories, and sketches. "His product was extensively subjective and his mood consistently depressed."

Most influential of all on Peter was Craig's suicide note (one of twelve), entitled simply, "Why?"

> Why?
> Because we see
> that people just
> won't do and say
> what they feel
> and you can't just

tell someone to.
It seems that
people are only
touched by death
and maybe people
will be touched
enough to look into
their lives
and if just one
person is touched
enough to do
something constructive
and peaceful with
their life then
maybe our death
was worth it.
Why — because we
love our fellow
man enough to
sacrifice our lives
so that they will
try to find the
ecstasy in just
being alive.

Love and peace,

Craig Badiali

Peter's last poem, "One Reason," was clearly modelled after Craig's:

Because everywhere I look
there is pain
and hunger
greed
and suffering

because I can't
take that
anymore.
Because maybe
by giving up my life
others will see
that they are blest
and they will see
that life
is a wonderful thing
and maybe
they will ask
why
are we killing one another?
and causing pain
and misery
and maybe
they will do something
about it.

At first glance the poems are strikingly similar in style and content. The style is unusual for Peter, who generally writes in iambic pentameter blank verse. Peter signs his suicide note the same way that Craig signs his. But these are just surface similarities. The poems are as different as their authors. The tone of Craig's is quiet and resigned, but strangely hopeful. Peter's poem is angry and bitter. He lashes out wildly and is logically inconsistent. If the world is as bad as he claims how will his death make people realize that life is beautiful when clearly it's not? And we know that it's Peter the moment he says, "I can't take it anymore." It's the same emotional resort of escape into death.

We can understand the despair and the motives for Craig and Joan's death, even if we disagree with them. They lived during a very turbulent time that was pulling their nation apart. The country was morally devastated; they felt their own values and future to be in jeopardy. How could they trust anything when their own country, that they had been brought up to believe in so strongly as the freest, most democratic nation in the world, committed to defending the democratic rights of others, was now perpetrating atrocities in some tiny, far-off land, all for the sake of protecting democracy? It was bewildering, frightening, disillusioning; and it touched them directly. Not only were young people they knew being called up to serve in a war they did not believe in, but soon Craig's turn would come. We can accept that Craig and Joan's suicide was a genuine, if misguided, effort to promote peace.

But Peter? What hunger, pain, suffering or greed did he know in the serene little town where he lived? What political issues was he protesting? What public cause was he dying for? If Peter sacrificed his life for anything it was for his own private hell. The terrible irony is that Peter never appreciated the futility of Joan and Craig's suicide; rather he was inspired by it, perhaps because he felt that it would ennoble his death by lending it some deep, martyred meaning. Therefore, he could not perceive the futility of his own suicide either.

Depression and fantasizing his own death become pleasures for him. It's his way of asserting his importance and his worth. In the world of death, he is king. He finds "freedom from his problems, freedom from his sisters and parents, freedom from the whole world," as did Retep Reklaw. But the danger of fantasizing is that he loses his grasp on reality. He orchestrates his funeral, lovingly and meticulously paying attention to all fine details. Not surprisingly, he wants *Strawberry Fields Forever* and *A Day in the Life* to be played at his funeral. (The latter describes a man who killed himself by blowing his brains out. Ironically, this is the only detail in the whole funeral scene that has a realistic touch.) He wants to be cremated and his ashes to be scattered in the wind or in the soil where he will "sprout each year and live forever." If life is ugly, he will fancifully make his own death beautiful. He imagines that his death will be as trouble free and enjoyable as his dream worlds. By detaching himself from his own death and viewing it as a spectator, he survives it. Death for him is just existence in another sphere.

146

Obviously, Peter doesn't recognize the finality of death. He views it as an adventure that he will survive and talk about. But in this respect he's not unique. It's not uncommon for many people who attempt suicide to be unaware of the irrevocable destruction they can bring upon themselves. One seventeen-year-old boy tried to kill himself by swallowing fifty aspirins; he documented his minute by minute feelings and body reactions:

6:05. It went down. Felt like throwing it up but didn't. Very upset stomach. Awful taste in mouth.
6:15. Stomach is gurgling. I wish it would hurry. If it doesn't I'm going to store to buy more aspirins.
6:35. Back from store. Just sweating. I'm about to take another twelve.
6:40. Heart seems to be beating harder, not faster. How can I take it so calmly?

He eventually gave up and had his stomach pumped, but in the interim he sat there matter-of-factly recording his body's reactions to the aspirins. The very real possibility that his life might soon end eluded him.

Peter's intense preoccupation with himself and his own end have an effect that he can scarcely appreciate. He doesn't realize that by dwelling so much on himself he cuts himself off even more from others, and the pain of his dilemma is intensified. One student who survived a suicide attempt was able to look back on his experience:

Only when I had made the attempt did I sense that one cannot die and do it again: that irrespective of any notions of immortality I could not command the attention of others in the state of my non-being. I have come to recognize that ...I may obscure the efforts of others to know me through too great an effort to know myself without the social context of relationships and interaction.[2]

What may have begun as a fantasy has by now been so rehearsed in his imagination that the suicide act itself has acquired a momentum of its own.[3] That's not to say that his suicide was inevitable, as Arlene, Jim, and Rita would like to think—perhaps to rationalize their own lack of involvement with him, and to assuage their guilt. Like almost all suicidal people, Peter vacillates between longings for life and longings for death. He had actually written a detailed suicide letter well over a year before his death, but he obviously changed his mind or at least delayed his action. His attitude remains ambivalent right up until the end. Nor is this unusual. A girl who tried to kill herself by drowning and was saved, quite by chance, later wrote:

I felt the water going into my mouth. I felt myself gagging. I pushed myself up and looked around me. It was as if I was seeing the world for the first time. I saw things that I never really noticed before. The sky was so blue, the birds seemed to be flying so freely in the sky. A million thoughts seemed to flash through my mind in those few seconds. God, I thought, it is a beautiful world and I am leaving it all behind. I felt the tears burning my eyes, and at the same time I prayed to God to help me. I gasped for air. I could not breathe. I was weak and tired. I gave up the struggle. I felt like I was going into a deep sleep that would last forever. Everything went black after that. When I woke up on the beach there was someone on top of me giving me artificial respiration.

I was grateful and thank God every day that I was saved.

In Peter the longings for death won out and there was no chance for intervention because he planned it that way. His suicide was more than a "cry for help."[4] It was a deafening roar that it was too late for that.

Any brave attempts he was making to let friends and teachers know how he felt brought no results. His friends clearly didn't know how to react. Jim knew that Peter had made a previous half-hearted attempt, but he didn't take it seriously.

Peter seemed much more cheerful after it. As for Peter's preoccupation with death, Jim just thought it was another of his academic interests – "He was always reading." And Arlene? She was terrified that Peter would do something, but she really didn't think he'd go that far. His friends just didn't know how to handle it. Like Peter, they were young and inexperienced. They didn't have a frame of reference for suicide. But what of his family and teachers?

He wrote a clearly suicidal story about Retep Reklaw (Peter Walker backwards) and handed it in to his English teacher along with some death poetry. All he got was a good grade. He showed the poetry and short story to his family, but they didn't take his meaning seriously. They figured he was just bright and a little morbid. He had even composed his final statement to the world – his detailed and more traditional suicide note[5] – and had even told his close friend Jim about a half-hearted suicide attempt he had made *well over a year before his death*. But he never got any response or reaction.

Was everyone deliberately choosing to ignore his messages? The answer that we hear over and over again from those who knew him and were close to him was that he just didn't seem depressed. Even Arlene who was actually afraid that he would do it put it out of her mind quite effectively because he just seemed so normal. Was it possible that he felt seriously depressed, but managed to act normal so that he succeeded in fooling everyone, even his parents? And if that were true, what would be his motive in fooling people when he readily admits that he's "crying for help"?

There is a growing body of literature that describes how to tell if someone is depressed and suicidal. Dr. Aaron T. Beck describes the three major signs of depressed people.[6] They think poorly of themselves and feel themselves powerless to change the situation. They have a negative view of the world and their relation to it. Third, they view the future with dread and pessimism. On the basis of Dr. Beck's theory we can view Peter as depressed, *but only through his writings*. In daily life he seems fine.

What about symptoms of suicide? A widely quoted pamphlet entitled "Dealing with the Crisis of Suicide" says:

> Many people contemplating suicide don't talk about it – especially the young, the elderly and professional persons – but they do go through periods of sleeplessness and general sadness. They may lose appetite, weight, sexual drive. They may lose interest in their work, in people and activities they once enjoyed.[7]

This certainly doesn't fit the description of a boy who ate, slept, was cheerful, did all his school assignments, and played hockey with his friends the night before he killed himself. The pamphlet continues:

> Another suicidal signal is preparation for death. A person may begin discussing insurance policies, or making a will, or giving away prized possessions.[8]

Of course this fits Peter, but only because we know about the farewell letter, which wasn't made public until *after* his death. It could never have been used as a clue for suicide.

Clearly then, there's a discrepancy between his behaviour and his writings. Arlene questions the integrity of the journals. She says that they were just "for show," implying that they don't reveal the true Peter. This view may have some element of truth but we can't accept it. To do so is to conclude that Peter was a bright, normal guy who killed himself for kicks and who left a bizarre journal deliberately to throw us off the track. Or else we have to see him as being deeply disturbed. We know that neither is true. We have to view his writings as desperate pleas to communicate that something was wrong. If that's not convincing enough, perhaps it's because Peter didn't know how to open himself up any more than he did. Or perhaps he just couldn't. Obviously he lacked the skills of Anne Frank and Alice's author that enabled them to unwittingly portray themselves as such real, likable people. Perhaps that is part of the hell he refers to in his suicide note, that he can't express feelings.

Why did he do it? Was he really too sensitive for this world, as his parents suggest? Was he ridden with guilt because of his sexual fantasies involving his sister? Or was it guilt because he resented the Indian kids yet wanted to help those that were suffering? Was it the baldness? Was it that he didn't get along with his parents? Was he terrified of the prospect of being a homosexual, as his last entry so blatantly denies? Was it school? Or God? "An act like this is prepared within the silence of the heart, as is a great work of art," said Camus of suicide.[9] It has a logic all its own that we will never understand. Surely, that's how Peter wanted it.

Peter's room is still exactly as he left it the day he died. In fact, everything is still pretty much the same, except that his parents will always grieve for him. His friends, in time, will forget. There are still hunger, greed, pain, and suffering in the world. Peter's death hasn't changed that. We may not know why he committed suicide, but we do know that his was a useless, senseless death.

6

THE SKELETON IN THE CLOSET

There are always two parties to a death; the person who dies and the survivors who are bereaved . . . the sting of death is less sharp for the person who dies than it is for the bereaved survivor. This, as I see it, is the capital fact about the relation between the living and the dying. There are two parties to the suffering that death inflicts; and in the apportionment of this suffering, the survivor takes the brunt.

Arnold Toynbee, Man's Concern with Death

Those people who were closest to Peter Walker describe how they have come to terms with his suicide:

Mrs. Walker

The first few weeks after Peter's death all I could do was weep and ask "Why? Why? It's so unfair." He was valued. I loved him so much. It didn't make sense that he would kill himself. Not the way he'd been treated. I felt that I was on trial, but that I was the judge and jury and witness, too. It's as if I was prosecuting myself and declaring myself guilty. I was almost completely out of touch with reality. I talked only to Peter, telling him how much I loved him. While the beautiful music was being played at his funeral, I had the weird thought of wondering what music Peter was listening to.

But our faith kept us strong, and I tried daily to become better, not bitter. I suppose my feelings were similar to most parents' in that situation in that I was seeking reassurance, especially from the other children that I had been a good mother. I know I had not neglected any aspect of their lives, and I usually knew where they were and what they were doing. When the children were small I was home all the time and I really enjoyed them and played with them. As they grew up I tried to keep up with what was going on in their lives and with others their age. I guess that's why it hurt so much when after Peter's death people tried to "comfort" us by telling us that he was crazy. I would have known!

It really hurt to read Peter write in his journal that he discovered that he was normal – just having weird thoughts, but writing them down. Then to go and destroy himself. With all the disease, retardation, and accidents in the world, it is a terrible shame to destroy a healthy body. He was a valuable human being that should never have been lost. I nearly get sick when I consider his potential.

I still think his death was unfair to himself and to his family. Did Peter really care more about people he never even knew than he did about his own family? I'm afraid I'm being judgemental. And I'm sad about negative thoughts being dominant. When young people think of killing themselves, do they also think how hurt a lot of people will be? If I could tell Peter a few things now I would question how much he cried over himself in the past year and how it compared with how much his brother and sisters cried over him in a week.

It finally dawned on me that our feelings and interpretations are a desperate attempt to have some message and some good come out of Peter's death. I guess our desire to share our story is part of the same thing. Also a lot of what Peter wrote was about making some good come of it. But he was certainly naive about grief. He never realized what loss meant because our family has been blessed and has not before now lost anyone.

I can cope with it now because I don't feel anymore that we were responsible. We did everything we could for Peter. We were the best parents we knew how to be. Sure he had problems, but it was up to him too to do something about them. We hadn't brought him up to think of death as the only solution; that was his way of handling things. We can only accept responsibility for our children up to a point. We have to let them make decisions and take responsibility for themselves, but it still affects us deeply and we are involved, no matter where they are.

A few weeks ago I was kneeling over the rose that we planted with some of his ashes and I thought, "Dear God. Is this all that's left?" And later I thought, "No. There's much more. We have the memories of a Peter who was warm, lively, intelligent, and funny. This is the Peter we have to remember to survive." My prayer is that Peter is with the Eternal Light and everlasting peace and love.

Mr. Walker

I could not be possessive over the life of my son. I feel that the makeup of a child is such an arbitrary, magical, miraculous haphazard thing, what with the arbitrary throwing together of chromosomes, that I couldn't possibly be responsible for the way that Peter turned out. I had done my best for him. I recognize now and I did then that he was different, sensitive, brilliant. But he just couldn't handle emotionally what he knew intellectually. I can't feel guilty for his death. I have the attitude, "The Lord gave, and the Lord hath taken away." I feel blessed that Peter was here with us on this earth for sixteen years.

154

Sandra

I've never lost anybody close to me before. I think a lot about the things we used to do together. In school I look around and I think, "Peter, you should be here. You should be with your friends. You should be going to the dance tonight." And he's not. And I find it hard to accept that he's never going to be around. I was writing a calculus test and I was thinking about Peter and I got mad. He never had to write exams. He never had to study hard or try to succeed in things. I keep thinking his suicide was like a cop-out. He could have done well in school.

I get mad. Everybody expects me to be so happy all the time. I guess they don't understand that the hurt's still here. They figure a month is all I'm allowed to be depressed. I find I have to smile or else everybody will think something's really gone wrong. Sometimes I hate the world because I'm not happy, but everyone else looks so happy. I miss Peter very much.

At home it's not the same. Somebody's missing all the time. At night I used to be able to go to sleep right away. I'd see Peter's light in the room across the hall and I'd feel safe. Sometimes I think that he's going to come walking through the door. And then I realize he's not going to, but it's hard to take that feeling away. I think about him all the time.

I'm very glad that he was here for sixteen years but I don't see why he couldn't be here for longer. I think that philosophy is good for Dad. It's what keeps him going. But it's not good for Mom. She does a lot of reading. She wants an answer, but she'll never get one.

But I've learned something from Peter's suicide. I've learned that there's a lot about a person inside that you may never know if you don't take the time to try and see beyond the face. I'd like to look around and see, is somebody treating someone else bad, and try and stop that, and try and help that person. No matter what, I just think that life is beautiful and that there is hope. And you must never give up and shut yourself away from people who could help you. And never, never could I think of committing suicide. I've seen so much hurt, and so much pain, I couldn't be responsible for any more.

Rita

I could feel guilty about it, but I can't live the rest of my life saying, "What if, what if?" Sometimes I feel bad that I didn't live at home last year, because maybe I could have helped him if I had known. And sometimes I get angry at his friends and teachers who read the death stuff that he was writing and didn't do anything; but then I figure, it wouldn't have mattered. The only thing anyone could have done was to have listened more.

I'm really happy now because I'm going to have a kid, and if it's a boy his middle name will be Peter. I don't want to call him Peter because that would lay too much of a trip on him, like when he hears about this guy Peter and what happened. I wouldn't want him to expect stuff. But my kid will be like me and I'm like Peter and that's good enough. We're Walkers. That really means a lot to me.

It wasn't that difficult for me to face people after Peter's death because I hang around mostly with the Indian population and they've had this happen to them many times before, and so they know how to react. All they can do is be there. But I think Sandra had a hard time because she was at school with his friends, kids that didn't even know him, but they knew what happened. So they're all kind of looking at her and passing judgement.

Jim

Since Peter I take death more seriously. The other day a friend of mine wanted to transfer schools. I saw him coming out of the guidance teacher's office. He had said no. David was really mad. He said, "I'm sick of this school. I should do like Peter did." I was pretty worried there for a while. I didn't want it to happen again. I watched him really carefully for a few days. But after a few days he snapped out of it.

I don't think I'd ever want to commit suicide. I have a pretty good time. Even considering some of the work we do at school. I only thought of that since Peter died. But I still can't help thinking that what he did was really stupid. He didn't accomplish a thing with his death, except to hurt people who were close to him.

Arlene

I can't talk to any of my friends about Peter. They just won't listen. You can only bring it up at certain times. Like, a lot of things I do I'm reminded of Peter. And I just want to say, "Peter would have done this like this," but I can't. I feel like they think, "She's just living in the past. He's dead now. Why doesn't she forget it?" But I can't. I don't think people understand it. You had to be close to Peter and not just forget. But a lot of people weren't close to him. They just knew him as a really nice guy who would help anybody, but that's all they knew him as.

I have to explain his suicide with love. It sounds kind of weird, I know, but when I think of him dying, I think of him dying because he loved us. He wanted us to see that life can be beautiful, if we'd make it like that. It's really illogical, but that's the way I think about it because I don't want to think about it any other way. He knew what he was doing, though. It was like premeditated murder.

I think about him every day and I want to love others, because I know that Peter wanted us to. I try to cover everything with love for him. It sort of dulls the pain, and it helps. But I miss him a lot. There are days I go into the library, and I say, "Oh, I'll go and talk to Peter." And he's not there. And it really hurts. Some days I feel like going somewhere and just sitting down and crying because I miss him so much, but I don't know if he'd want me to. Maybe I should just keep on living.

Today we got our yearbooks. One of my friends wrote, "Life is beautiful and we have to keep on living." I just hugged him and said, "Thanks." I have to be reminded of that.

157

Of all situations involving a death, survivors of a suicide surely have the most difficult task of coping, for suicide is a wilful, deliberate death. Even in such unexpected tragedies as Hiroshima, where parents had no power whatsoever in preventing their children's deaths, they nonetheless felt guilty that they were unable to do so.

Children's deaths had particularly strong impact, whatever the circumstances. These aroused in parents a special kind of guilt associated with failure to carry out the most fundamental psycho-biological tasks in caring for the young – giving life to them and maintaining them in it. Parents' later self-reproaches had more to do with these basic emotions than with the actual details of a child's death, which in fact, they often reconstructed in a way that made them the most culpable.[1]

When a child dies because of illness, the effect on the parents can be devastating. Frequently they wonder whether some wrong they have committed could have caused the child's illness.[2] Or they are tormented by the thought that they didn't do enough to save the child. The grief can become so intense that the very existence of the survivor is in jeopardy. One mother, whose ten-year-old son died after surgery performed to correct a heart defective from birth, described it this way:

There was a period after Robby died when I floated and just went through the mechanical motions of cooking and cleaning and holding banal conversations. It was a time of numbness. Conversely, it was a time when the pain was so intense it was actually physical. I recall feeling that I had undergone the amputation of a leg or arm.

It was then I experienced my greatest fear as a survivor. Horrified and frozen, I used to think, what if it would always be like this? What if the pain never stopped? The thought of endless days spent in a quicksand of grief pulling me farther and farther down from any semblance of normalcy frequently panicked me.

Eventually, though, after a few months, both the panic and physical pain subsided and I felt reassured I would survive. It was only then I decided I actually wanted to.[3]

If death of children through uncontrollable forces can evoke such feelings of guilt and despair in survivors, then it is easy to understand how detrimental a force suicide can actually be for survivors. Frequently it is a death for which the family is totally unprepared. "The more unexpected the death, the more acute and disturbing the grief."[4] And suicide represents the ultimate rejection. Implicit in an adolescent's suicide is the judgement that his family and friends were not able to help him with his problems, and were certainly incapable of helping him find happiness. He is also telling them that he doesn't value them enough to stick around.

The guilt and shame of survivors can be ferocious. Because suicide is a deliberate act, they feel responsible for it:

The bereaved person searches the days before the death of the lost one looking for evidences of his own failure to do all that he might to ensure the latter's survival. He accuses himself of negligence and overemphasizes minor omissions. He may look for a scapegoat and blame doctors and nurses and other members of the family for not having done all they could to preserve life or contribute to the happiness and comfort of the loved one.[5]

Most of all, though, the survivor blames himself. Why didn't he pay more attention to the signs? He feels as guilty as if he himself had pulled the trigger.

The reaction of the community doesn't help either. Invariably, the family is blamed. The usual logic is, "If they had been good parents, the kid wouldn't have wanted to kill himself. They made him do it." They are branded forever. To compound the difficulties, there also appears to be a social reaction to suicide. Frequently, a family mourning a suicide will not receive emotional support from friends and relatives, who find it impossible to talk about the deceased and do not help the mourners in accepting their loss.[6] It's as if suicide is a terrible disease and they don't wish to be contaminated. As a result, the family finds itself more isolated and adrift.

They become hostile at the very mention of suicide. Two psychiatrists who undertook to study parents whose adolescent children had committed suicide, reported that they had extreme difficulty in doing so:

> As we entered the lives of these parents, we upset their tenuous defensive equilibrium. They became anxious and angry at us. Our letters went unanswered, telephones were banged in our ears, appointments were broken and both bodily and legal threats were made to keep us away from spouses and children ... These were the extremes. However, even those parents who accepted the interview expressed displeasure and hostility towards anyone who called their child's death a suicide.[7]

It is this attitude, and the shame that it engenders, that leads to the widespread under-reporting of suicides. Families frequently make frantic efforts to minimize both unsuccessful suicide attempts and, especially, successful suicides.[8] Their unwillingness to deal with the suicide can be extremely destructive. An essential part of the mourning process – indeed a sign that the process is complete – is an acceptance of death. "Denial, concealment, refusal or inability to talk about the suicide tend to freeze or halt the mourning process in its earliest stages."[9] There is always the danger that the survivor can become so overwhelmed with guilt and depression that suicide seems the only proper end. Or else the legacy is a threat of doom, the feeling that "My brother killed himself. Is that what's in store for me?"[10] Siblings are particularly vulnerable, not only because they feel guilty, but because often they are cut off by their own parents, who are too absorbed by their own guilt and grief to pay any meaningful attention to their surviving children.[11]

The emotional responses to suicide, both by the immediate family and the community at large, serve only to intensify and multiply the problems inherent in suicide. Taboos, guilt, and blame do nothing to promote a sympathetic understanding and a supportive openness of feeling that are essential to the wellbeing and wholeness of the survivors.

Because of the attitude to suicide in our society, I knew when I began writing this book that to find and interview the parents of an adolescent who had succeeded in killing himself would be very difficult. In fact, two years of research had convinced me that it would be next to impossible. The closest I had ever come was a series of lengthy telephone conversations with one mother; she just couldn't face me for a personal interview. Others didn't even want to talk about it on the phone. It wasn't hard to conclude that the guilt, shame, and pain surrounding the suicide of a child rendered it a subject too painful to talk about with a stranger, or perhaps anyone, even a year or two after the death had occurred. I continued to search, but not with great optimism.

One day I received a letter from a woman who had read in a newspaper that I was writing a book on adolescent suicide. She wrote that her teenaged son had killed himself, and she hoped that "our story might be of help to disturbed, confused youth. We do want to help in some way (and be helped too)." She invited me to come to their town to talk to them.

I did eventually go to the town where she lived. I talked extensively with her, her husband, and her daughters. She arranged for me to meet her son's friends. She showed me his journals and poetry. Nothing was hidden. There was no shame, no hostility; only sadness, deep love, guilt, and great bewilderment as to why the suicide had occurred. The result is the story of Peter Walker.

If the Walkers had any personal motives in offering to share their story it was that they wanted an explanation of why Peter had killed himself, and they wanted assurances that he wasn't crazy. Some people, in an attempt to comfort them, had assured them that the suicide wasn't their fault; it was Peter's, because he had been mentally ill, they said. One psychologist

161

told them that from reading Peter's journal he judged him to be schizophrenic. These labels, particularly the psychologist's, upset the Walkers terribly – because they viewed him as an authoritative figure. They wanted to maintain a memory of Peter that was as flawless as possible. To have him diagnosed as crazy was to mar that precious image and to heighten their guilt: if their son and brother was really disturbed, as so many said he was, then what was wrong with them, his closest family, that they hadn't noticed?

I could not satisfy either motive. I couldn't tell them why Peter had killed himself, and I couldn't tell them whether or not Peter was crazy. However, I could tell them that many young people I had talked to who had attempted suicide were, in my estimation, far from crazy. On the contrary, they were like Peter – bright, perceptive, sensitive, and introspective.

From the moment they found out about Peter's death, the Walkers behaved with great courage and honesty. There was never any hesitation in admitting that Peter's death was caused by his own hand. Never was any emotion spent on deception. Four days after he died, a memorial service was held for Peter to which all who knew him and his family were invited to attend. Several days later his father prepared a mimeographed letter that was sent to their many friends and scattered relatives. The letter contained an announcement of Peter's death and excerpts from his journal. And it was only six weeks after Peter's death that Mrs. Walker first contacted me: Peter's suicide was never hushed up.

No one would dispute that Peter's death hurt his family deeply. But the fact that they did not waste precious emotional energy concealing his suicide helped ensure their survival of the tragedy that so unexpectedly befell them. Another factor that helped them survive was their ability to express anger.

It is common for one of the initial reactions of survivors to be anger. That feeling comes of having been abandoned and publicly shamed. "If he really loved us, how could he have left us? How could he have embarrassed us in this way?" These are frequently expressed sentiments, but they usually don't last. They are replaced by terrible guilt and self-recriminations. The survivors tend to ennoble and almost deify the dead person, while at the same time reducing their own worth, because they were powerless to prevent his death. It's very easy to fall into that predicament, because in our culture, speaking ill of the dead is strictly forbidden.

It's crucial that the survivors do not feel unjustified guilt. The mother whose son died after heart surgery came through because she was able to avoid this pitfall. As she said:

> I credit in large measure my lack of feeling unjustified guilt to having followed their [her son's doctors'] advice. I take comfort in knowing my son had as normal a childhood as his poor health and its frequent incursions upon his life would allow.[12]

In short, she had done everything she could.

The Walkers were able to keep things in perspective. Mr. Walker realized that ultimately he had no control over his son; Mrs. Walker was able to express legitimate negative feelings about Peter because he had chosen death as a solution. Both parents accepted the fact that they were not responsible for his self-inflicted death. Jim and Sandra, too, were able to say openly that they viewed Peter's death as a cop-out. Rita realized that "if onlys" were useless. Arlene expressed no negative feelings, but perhaps she didn't have the need to. For the survivors to pull through they have to view the dead person realistically, as he was in life, as a person with both good and bad qualities who didn't have the fighting spirit to get him through. If those left behind after a death do, indeed, get the brunt of the suffering, then they must adopt the fighting attitudes of survival.

7

CAN THIS STORY HAVE A HAPPY ENDING?

We demonstrate to anyone whose soul has fallen to pieces that he can rearrange these pieces of a previous self in what order he pleases, and so attain to an endless multiplicity of moves in the game of life. As the playwright shapes a drama from a handful of characters, so do we from the pieces of the disintegrated self build up ever new groups, with ever new interplay and suspense, and new situations that are eternally inexhaustible.
Herman Hesse, Steppenwolf

Linda

Everything I did was criticized as a child. You're talking too loud or too much. Even Kool-Aid — Don't spill it. You're drinking too fast or too much. You can only have one glass. Don't be a pig. Things like that. It was a constant harping. I'd go out and play all day to avoid it, and then I'd get shit for not coming back home. "Where were you? I was worried." But they couldn't care less. They were busy or sleeping or something.

Starting from very young, it was my father working and my mother working also, and I was raised by my grandmother. She was a fine, powerful woman who understood children, but everyone else was afraid of her. My mother really disliked this woman who had taken over her child and handled her so well. My grandmother was very good with me and never made me feel bad about anything. She died when I was eight; that was the end of my life.

When my mother was around I could never do anything right. She worked all day and came home with a headache. You had to be quiet. If I lost a button off a blouse I would get a smack because that was being careless. Or if I was really dirty I'd get a licking. This was something I wasn't used to. My grandmother would have said, "Clothes can be washed, have fun." Around that time my father lost interest in me. Things got bad for him and he started drinking. Typical Irish alcoholic. I'm terrified of him as was my mother.

At first I reacted to that. But all I got was, "Shut up. You have nothing to say. You have no rights. You're a child." It was hard for me to adjust to, because always before I had lots to say. I was always listened to.

Even when I got sick they'd be mad at me. I used to get bronchial pneumonia when I was a kid. My mother would just be furious. She'd say, "If you hadn't gotten your feet wet that wouldn't have happened to you." Then she'd come home from work and shout at me because I hadn't done the dishes. Well the reason I hadn't done the dishes was that I was told to stay in bed and not move because she didn't want me sick any longer. And if I got out of this bed I was going to be in big trouble. So it was a terrible circle that I could just never get out of. I was very frightened all the time. I tried to bring attention to myself in any possible way. I used to think if I'd step out in front of a car I'd get hurt and not killed; they'd be sorry, and everyone would like me. I was about ten when I started thinking that.

I don't remember any love or affection in my house other

165

than the time when my mother needed affection herself. She's an affectionate woman; she needs love. We'd watch television and cuddle together. But those times were few and far between. But things that other kids do — like baking together — it was much quicker for my mom to do it herself. You know how it is. You've got a little kid. You've got to show them everything. It's really faster to do it yourself. She really didn't have time to show me things and be with me.

Then my little brother was born when I was thirteen and that was the greatest thing in my life. Still is. But he caused a lot of extra work. He became my responsibility. Less than five months after my mother had him she was out to work again. The house was my responsibility. That was fine, but I also needed time to play, which I didn't have. That was unfortunate. There was also a lot of jealousy from my mother. This child didn't know her, but he was her son. We also had a great aunt come to live with us. She was eighty-six, getting senile, and she became my responsibility too. So I had a little child, old aunt, school, and a house.

My father was out really drinking now. He'd come home and just be impossible. He'd come home at five in the morning, drunk. My mother, being so afraid of him, would let him make me go out and look for his car. I was only thirteen.

It was just a household full of hate, and it still is. Dinner table was just eat, get up, do the dishes, and be quiet. I used to spend all my time in my room. I started lying just for self-preservation. I'd want to play basketball, but I knew if I told my parents they wouldn't let me. So I started lying. Saying that I had to work extra time after school, just so I could play. I didn't want to take the chance of them saying no. It was ridiculous. Some of the things that I lied about I shouldn't have had to lie about, but I thought I did because I was so frightened.

I was so frightened to say that I had failed. I was working weekends and three nights a week at a store. I got laid off — not fired. I was too scared to tell them. I went out every night that I was supposed to be working and pretended to be working. When they found out they were furious. They shook me and screamed, "Why do you do this? What's the matter with you?" *I'm too scared to tell you. That's what.* Of course I didn't say that. I just sat there shrugging my shoulders.

I was always running around, trying to calm things down in the house. If the baby was making noise I'd grab him and run outside to play; I had to because if he disturbed them they'd get angry and they'd get angry at me. The great aunt had trouble turning the taps off. There's nothing my father would get so angry about for some reason as the taps. I used to run after her every time she used the bathroom and turn the taps off. That would be the first thing I'd do. I'd run home in between classes to turn the taps off! It sounds ridiculous. It is ridiculous. But then it was real.

When I went into the hospital I was hallucinating and in one of my hallucinations there was my father screaming about the taps, and I was crying, "I didn't turn them on, I didn't turn them on." The guilt sort of builds in you. You spend so much time trying to keep things running smoothly so there are no flare-ups, but it doesn't matter. Whatever you do, it's not going to come out right.

You have to understand that my mother is unhappy, and a little mentally ill I think. She needs help, too. This was her problem. The only way she could punish us was to make us feel guilty. You were always feeling badly about something. There was never a day you felt good.

It went to the point where it was ridiculous, where it was all in my own mind. If my parents had an argument I blamed myself. When anything happened, it was my fault. Even if it wasn't my fault, I could have stopped it, so it was my fault. So I couldn't win. I don't think they actually blamed me for many things I blamed myself for, but it was ingrained in me.

When I was sixteen, I was going to school and working in a nursing home, feeding old ladies, washing floors, doing laundry. Not a great job; but I really enjoyed it. I liked the old ladies. And I had my little brother and my great aunt. But I had no time to do anything. No time to go out. I wasn't allowed to go out anyway. If you were out past nine o'clock you're out with *boys*.

I just hated myself so much by then that I started hallucinating. It started coming back on me. All the anger and everything that was inside came back in hallucinations, voices. No one in the room, but six people talking to me. I didn't drink — I was too afraid to — and it wasn't drugs by any means. It was just my own mind turning on me. Then of course it seemed real. I was too confused and depressed then to know what was happening. The voices were just there. I listened to them. They hated me. It was me hating me. They would go on for hours about what a rotten person I was, until I took it as a fact. I'm no good. I never will be. I might as well accept it. And I'll just cause everybody trouble. That's all.

I was so unhappy and so confused. I guess it was what you'd call a mental breakdown. I didn't know what I was wearing when I went to school. My mind would be a blank, and wander off somewhere. I couldn't do anything properly. I was having nightmares. I'd wake up outside at night. My mother took sleeping pills; she never heard me. I used to wander back in by myself. It got so I was afraid to go to sleep. So without sleep and with these voices and everything else on my mind, I just cracked.

My mother sent me to the doctor because I was "not myself" and he gave me some nerve pills, but I was afraid to tell her. My mother took nerve pills and I knew they were bad. I had all these cards of nerve pills that the doctor had given me as samples so I wouldn't have to go out and buy them. I just hadn't been taking them. Every time I went to the doctor he'd give me more, but I didn't tell him that I wasn't taking them. I didn't want him to know that I wasn't following orders. I liked having the pills there, though. They gave me a feeling of importance. "I have bad nerves." That was my excuse. "Something is wrong."

Anyway I didn't plan the suicide attempt. It was just that there were all these voices and I was completely taken over. I wasn't in control. Maybe subconsciously I did want to die or else these voices wouldn't have been telling me to take the pills. But in my own self I wasn't planning it. What would my brother and auntie do without me? So I went home and took them.

There were problems at school too: Not having the right clothes. Not having the right attitude to be popular. And I had those normal teenage problems like acne and being flat chested. There was no escape. I didn't fit anywhere.

There was no real great thing that made me decide to go out and kill myself the next day. It was just the final day. I can't take any more and that's it. And that's how I cracked. So I took an overdose. I took about fifty strong tranquillizers. A counsellor at school who had noticed that I had problems (I had never talked to her, though) because I was so obviously depressed, saw me leaving school and realized in the middle of the afternoon that I wasn't there. She phoned my great-aunt who told her that she couldn't wake me up. She raced over and brought me directly to the hospital. If not for her I'd be dead today.

I woke up a couple of days later and my parents were there. They couldn't understand why I had done it. They didn't know that anything was wrong. It's amazing because everyone else did. But they didn't know that something was wrong with me. My father was insisting that he take me out. So the staff committed me to a psychiatric ward. They let me out a month later.

My parents were just amazed and frightened by the whole thing. They were blaming themselves, and anybody else they could lay their hands on. And also blaming me. And I was blaming myself for hurting them so badly and for adding another stress. So as soon as I got out I walked in front of a truck.

In the month I was in the hospital my parents were there every night. My school acquaintances — I can't call them friends — showed up in hordes; I had thirty kids in my room the first night. A new place to go. Something different. This wasn't in their experience. They came up for a couple of weeks and never came up again.

My mother was coming every night. And that was another added thing. She didn't have time. She worked. Now there was no one to look after my brother and my aunt, and here she was having to come up to the hospital every night. She was always crying. I was pretty sick-looking and depressed. So I'd feel badly and try to put up a front for her. I did get a good front going after a couple of weeks: I was cheerful, running around helping the nurses, planning every moment that the day that I get out I'm going to do it right this time. And they let me out. They were quite pleased with my recovery. The doctors said maybe it was a teenage boyfriend, some puppy love that depressed me and I thought I'd get some attention by taking pills. And of course it wasn't that at all. The day I got out, there I was trying again. I walked out in front of a truck.

So I got in a second time. This time they let me out in six months, but I was on a lot of pills. And I started hallucinating again. But these were not bad hallucinations. Like I'd walk up to the closet and slap something. Gotcha! (I don't remember this at all. My mother told me.) I'd be up all night, awake. Making breakfast at two in the morning for everybody. Waking them all up. "Come on, it's time to eat." I never slept. My mother had to follow me everywhere because she just didn't know what I was going to do. I was completely gone. Like in a story. Except that this is my story. After a few days of that she just couldn't handle me anymore. So she just had to take me back. I don't remember getting back into the hospital. I was just there.

They gave me shock treatments and fifteen pills a day. They didn't look at any problems that I had. They just covered them up with pills so I didn't feel anything any more. And the shock treatments were to help the depression. But I still had the depression somehow. I had already gone through two psychiatrists by this time. I was on the third one who said, "There's nothing we can do. Off she goes to the state mental hospital." That's when the general hospital here in town stepped in and said, "We've got a new youth service." So there I went for a year.

The whole time I was in the first hospital nobody tried to deal with my problems. They just tried to subdue me with pills. I saw a psychiatrist once a week and it wasn't even for an hour. He'd only pop in and wave. Sometimes he'd speak to you. But he never really spoke to you. He'd just tell you what they were going to do with you next. The nurses were supposed to be writing down on charts what was happening to you. But they had to do everything in there. Even the cleaning. They didn't have time. There weren't enough of them. I think they used to make things up pretty well. They used to watch what you ate, things like that. If you didn't eat your supper you were depressed. And sometimes if you did eat your supper and you ate lots you were even more depressed. You just couldn't win in there either.

When I attempted suicide I really wanted to die. I wanted it over with. I didn't want any more life. No more. And thinking that I'd only be trouble wherever I went, I didn't want to be into anything else. I deserved to die. I meant to die. I wasn't just making gestures saying, "I'm unhappy, pay attention to me." I had done all my attention-getting before. I used to hit myself and get great big bruises so someone would say, "Hey, did you hurt yourself?" I would never hide any illnesses. If I was sick I was really sick. Come in and care for me a little bit. But it didn't work out. But all the attention-grabbing had been done. I'd done everything I could.

At the general hospital they didn't pump me up full of pills. I was addicted partially to one drug, I'd been taking it for so long. They took me off most drugs. They gave me some just to keep me at a point where I could deal with my problems. I wasn't just a robot. They talked to me when I started hallucinating, and I used to hallucinate regularly. "The house was on fire!" I really believed that there was something happening to my brother and I must go to him. I nursed him and I guess I felt he needed me. I was packing my clothes all the time to go, and every time I did it they gave me a needle and I'd go to sleep.

They talked me down from these things. They'd sit there, and they'd sit there for hours if necessary, and say, "Okay, there are no voices. Talk to me. What are you feeling?" At first you'd be hysterical. But you'd have to talk. But then sooner or later you calm down without drugs. They tried to get my parents in for group therapy. It didn't work out. My father got insulted and left the very first time. There was nothing wrong with him! He never came again. My mother came but she had all these great problems: I never did anything to help her. I was always causing trouble. It wasn't her fault. That's what she kept screaming all the time. She didn't deserve to have this happen to her. I guess it's natural. She was just protecting herself. I don't think I was the easiest person to live with either. I was pretty depressed. I was no joy to a mother's heart. I would just slink around the house. I don't blame her at all. Group therapy was a total loss. We cut that out and never did it anymore.

After about a year I was out again and got a job. I didn't sleep at the hospital. I just spent all day there and slept at home. That made a difference because I couldn't run away from my problems. I always had to go to them. The hospital was a place I could lean on, but it wasn't a complete escape. I had to deal with it. I had to talk about it and let them help me with it. It's a good thing that they did it that way.

I got better through the talking. I started to believe in myself again. Finally I just got sick of going to that hospital. I hated it because someone was always working on my mind or telling me what to do. "It's time for occupational therapy or psychodrama." (That's where you play out hostilities.) You can't live like that. I wanted to be out doing what I wanted. I was getting older. I was working on my problems.

I still have problems I'm working on, especially anger. It's not even that I can't express it, I can't even identify it or recognize feeling it sometimes. It's usually "you've hurt me," not "you've made me angry." I feel hurt that you've done this to me. It somehow comes back on me. I always feel that if I hadn't done something wrong they wouldn't feel this way. My therapist puts things into perspective.

My first job was in a dairy store. Then I got in at the telephone company. From there into a receptionist. I learned typing and accounting at another job. I went from job to job, learning as I went along.

Working and just getting a pay cheque gave me confidence. The money meant "you've done a good job this week." That was a big push.

Today I really feel sorry for my parents. Their lives haven't changed. My mother's in very bad shape. She's very unhappy. My father's very unhappy. But they won't split for the sake of the children. I do visit often, but I don't like it. I bother because I want to be a good daughter. I still have guilt feelings. My mother phones me constantly asking me to do things, and no matter what I do I can never do them right. I'm still a sore point in her life because I moved out.

I'd like to write them off. I've had death wishes for them — and felt guilty. I've often hated them. But I can't write them off. I love them, for some stupid reason.

I've been told that the more a child is rejected the more he'll try to win the parents' love. But it never does any good. I hope that won't be me.

If I lived with them they'd probably destroy me. It doesn't get to me as much because I don't live with them.

I've got to think, my mother's ill. That's really true, not just my way of dealing with the problem. She's a martyr. Masochistic to a point that it's an illness. It's enraging what she'll put up with. Her mother treated her the same way she treats me and still treats her that way. And I have a tendency to put guilt on other people — like in a fight with my boyfriend. But I know that I'm doing it so I try not to.

I've come a long way and I could never have made it without the excellent help that I finally got. But do you realize how close I came to being a lunatic for life?

Figures don't lie. In the last twenty years in both the US and Canada the suicide rate for people ages fifteen to twenty-four has almost tripled.[1] [2] But that figure doesn't even begin to reveal the magnitude of the problem. For every adolescent who makes a successful suicide attempt it has been estimated that there are sixty to one hundred who try and fail.[3] And for all those who attempt it unsuccessfully how many are there who contemplate it? Talk to any person who works in an emergency room of a major hospital. Talk to any high school or university teacher. Talk to any teenager. Statistics convey very little.

Whatever the causes, whatever the figures, suicide is preventable. For the dead there is no hope. As long as a person is alive, no matter how troubled or self-destructive he may be, there is always the chance that he can be helped to find better ways of dealing with his problems, that he can be taught to live again. We are morally bound to take up that challenge – the stories of all the young people in this book should convince us of that.

If this may seem self-evident to many people, there are those who would argue that we have no right to interfere when someone wants to take his own life. We may be tempted to scoff at people who hold such views and write them off as unfeeling people who are unfamiliar with the problems of suicide. But when that view is expressed by a psychiatrist of some prominence we sit up and take notice.

Thomas Szasz is such a psychiatrist. He believes that the psychiatrist should not intervene if a patient wants to take his own life. Aside from the fact that it is an infringement of his civil liberties, the patient will manipulate the psychiatrist by threatening suicide if he knows that he can get him to respond when he makes such threats. This is a deterrent to effective treatment. " . . . Only if the patient is deeply convinced that the analyst respects his autonomy, including his right to take his own life, can he engage effectively in the analytic exploration and mastery of his ideas about suicide."[4] What he leaves out is that the greatest deterrent to effective treatment is a dead patient.

Szasz says that the main reason that physicians and other mental health professionals declare themselves ready and willing to help suicidal patients is because they perceive suicide as a threat to themselves and their value system, and so they strike back. "This explains why psychiatrists and suicidologists resort, apparently with a perfectly clear conscience, to the vilest methods: they must believe that their lofty ends justify the basest means. Hence the prevalent use of force and fraud in suicide prevention."[5]

Szasz's theory would be tenable if all people who sought help from their psychiatrists were rational and capable of clear judgement. Then Szasz might say to such a patient, "As long as you are undergoing treatment with me you must understand that you can never make a suicidal threat to me in any way. If you want to take your life that's your business. I'm not responsible." And the patient might say, "Of course. I agree to the terms of the contract. Now get on with the business of analysing." But most people who seek psychiatric help, and especially adolescents, are unsuitable candidates for such an agreement. They are depressed, perhaps hopeless, and they can't cope. What they need is help, not a lecture on contracts. And if they are helped they can learn to overcome the problems that were incapacitating them, and lead meaningful lives. Surely Howard, Lenore, Bill, Bruce, and Linda would agree.

If we need any further convincing that troubled lives are worth saving we might refer back to the girl in Chapter One who wanted someone to pull the plug on her to put her out of her misery. She was sixteen at the time. Two years later she sent the following Christmas card to her therapist:

Just thought this would be a good time to send a little hello. I figure this is the best time to thank you for everything you have done for me, because without you, I couldn't be what I am today. Sure I still have problems and I still have hang-ups, but I have changed to a more happy and fulfilled person. Thank you again. I shall always remember you and how much you did for me. Thank you a million times. May God bless you and your family for the rest of your lives. Merry Christmas and a Happy New Year.

Suicide, then, can and must be prevented. But how? As we have seen from all the people whose stories we have read, suicidal people give signs of their intentions – strong signs. A suicidal person may express his intention verbally by saying simply, "I'm going to kill myself." He may show it through his behaviour by becoming withdrawn, depressed, and uncommunicative. He may not eat or sleep well. There may be a sharp drop in his school performance. Adolescents who are depressed may act out their depression by becoming restless or delinquent. When he feels the end is near, a suicidal person may write a will, distribute farewell notes, or give away prized possessions, as Peter did. And of course a previous suicide attempt is a strong warning. Four out of five persons who kill themselves have attempted to do so at least once previously.[6]

Another signal is a general feeling of hopelessness. One woman who works with teenagers in a community drop-in centre described it this way: "When a kid is going through a bad time I ask him how he feels about the future. If he says that he knows that he's going through a bad time now but that things will get better, I relax a little. If he tells me he's without hope I'm always on the lookout for suicide." Indeed, studies have shown that hopelessness defined in terms of negative expectations is the strongest indication of suicidal intent, stronger even than depression.[7]

Any person showing any of these signs should be taken seriously. To laugh it off as a joke, to brush it aside as a mere attention-getting device, or merely to tell the person not to say those things or to behave in that way is to miss an opportunity to save a life, and later to find oneself saying, "I didn't believe she was serious," or "I never thought he'd really do it."[8] It's so easy to react the way Peter's family, friends and teachers did; but it's impossible to undo the results of those reactions.

Does this mean that any person exhibiting any of these signs is suicidal? No. But it does mean that that person is unhappy, has problems, and could do with some help, even if he's not asking for it directly. The difficulty is to know how to provide that help. We might often feel ill-equipped or uncomfortable doing it. The most important thing to do is to show the person that we're concerned about him and that we care. If we can't provide the help ourselves we shouldn't abandon the person just because we are powerless to furnish the solutions. We should contact his parents or teachers, anyone who is close to him and has some influence over him, or we should encourage him to get help from any counselling service that may exist in the community. In short, we should take action.

A person who is depressed, particularly a young person who may not have experienced serious depression before, needs to have the assurance that he is not crazy. As Peter, Howard,

Bruce, and Liz have amply proven to us, the fear of being considered insane can make a situation much worse than it actually is. To be sure, there are therapists who consider a suicidal teenager to be mentally ill. "The emotionally healthy adolescent does not either commit suicide or attempt to do so. One cannot escape the fact that the teenager who tries to kill himself is emotionally disturbed."[9] There are other therapists, however, who are able to deal with a suicidal adolescent without attaching damning labels to him. The director of a crisis intervention unit of a large metropolitan hospital sees it this way:

The "typical" suicidal patient of my own clinical experience is, however, not "insane" in either a psychiatric or legal sense of the word. He is a person with problems – not one problem, but a series of them. Emotional resources have been strained to their limit and coping becomes more and more difficult. The individual senses that he is caught in a trap, that it is futile to struggle on. Other people don't seem to understand or appreciate his plight. Emotion becomes heightened and with it, a certain tunnel-vision effect as far as problem resolution is concerned. Options may exist, but they are not seen. Instead, thoughts of another way out become more and more frequent. At first these thoughts are pushed away, but then something else goes wrong and it's just too much. The suicidal act itself may be impulsive. The first attempt usually is. It is a confused, angry, frightened, desperate act.[10]

The resources available to a suicidal person vary depending on where he lives, his family, and, of course, himself. Most major cities in the US and Canada have crisis lines that are manned on a twenty-four hour basis. They provide immediate, anonymous, sympathetic counselling. The lines are generally served by volunteers who have been carefully trained in handling crisis situations. Often it is comforting and useful just to talk to someone who will listen. Some centres are limited to telephone counselling alone; others have "outreach" services where face-to-face follow-up meetings can be set up. Some also have emergency vehicles that can be dispatched at a moment's notice. The drawbacks to a distress line are that the line may be busy, and the person in trouble has to initiate the activity. But surely the latter drawback applies to almost any service that will ultimately provide help. Lenore and Diane are alive today to tell their stories because of distress centres.

Some cities have walk-in or drop-in clinics where anyone in need can come in off the street, usually without an appointment, and talk to a trained counsellor. The importance of being able to find help at the time one feels it is needed is crucial. To have to force a problem to fester inside when it needs to be brought out into the open can be extremely detrimental. Many tragedies could be averted if more of these immediate services were available.

The necessity for immediate help is nowhere as apparent as in emergency rooms of hospitals. A person who has attempted suicide and is brought to a hospital usually requires two types of treatment: one for his body and one for his mind. Too often, all a hospital can and will provide is physical care, and even that is given grudgingly by nurses and doctors who may be unsympathetic and even hostile to suicidal people. They consider them a nuisance. One doctor offered this opinion: "I can't be bothered with them. They take up my time when I could be helping someone else who really wants to live." This attitude not only wrongly assumes that people who attempt suicide aren't interested in living, but it betrays extreme hostility. Nor is this doctor unique in his attitude.
Why is this?

The best explanation is in terms of the attitudes that medical training seems to instil. Medical personnel see themselves responding to the needs of the victim – the innocent victim – be it of motor vehicle accident or of dog bite. They serve patients with genuine needs who are grateful to the doctor for using his skills to aid them. To medics, the suicidal person is, by these criteria, all wrong. He does not play the doctor-patient game. He is trying to throw away the life that the sensible patient fights to maintain, the life that the doctor has pledged himself to preserve. Furthermore, the suicidal person is not properly appreciative of the medical measures taken on his behalf and, of course, there is always the threat that after the doctor has gone to all the time and effort of saving his wretched life, the suicidal individual may go out and make another attempt to throw it away. That kind of "craziness" does not elicit much sympathy.[11]

To be fair, most hospitals aren't equipped to do more than look after a suicidal patient's immediate physical needs. What is required is on-the-spot counselling and comforting (assuming of course that the person is conscious). The Toronto East General Hospital, for example, has a Crisis Intervention Unit which has trained volunteers in the emergency room twenty-four hours a day, seven days a week, to deal with the immediate emotional needs of people in suicidal crisis. Says Dr. Diane Syer, the director of the unit:

You have to get to basics with someone who has just attempted suicide. And the basic thing is that they don't want to die. That's the common denominator of the failed suicidal act. If they say, "I don't want to die. Help me." you don't ask them to tell you about their mother or their childhood experiences. You just respond to what they're saying, to their emotional needs of the moment. You respond by saying, "I don't want you to die either. I care about what's happening to you. If I can help I'll do everything I can." The person may never have heard that, and that's what's important at that moment.

Unfortunately in many hospitals in North America such a service is not available. Instead, what often happens is that the person who has attempted suicide may be given an appointment with a psychiatrist or a social worker for a week later. By that time the person is so ashamed or so deeply depressed that the likelihood of his keeping that appointment is small. Nothing has been solved.

The people in this book who have told their stories have come down hard on psychiatrists and their methods. We have only heard their side, which is not objective; and of all medical specialists it is perhaps easiest to malign psychiatrists. But that is because they deal with human emotions (people don't get very upset about their osteopaths, for example). In forcing patients to come to terms with their problems psychiatrists may also arouse their hostility. In their efforts to probe they run the risk of offending those who are sensitive. And some people become very defensive just at the thought of getting involved in therapy because they may feel it confirms the fact that they are indeed crazy.

So the dynamics involved in a patient-psychiatrist relationship can be very complex. They may be further complicated if the psychiatrist feels uncomfortable with a suicidal person. As Szasz has already pointed out, people in the helping professions may feel threatened by a person who attempts suicide because he defies what they value, namely life. Fortunately there are many who react by committing themselves to keeping that person alive, or at least to attempting to do so. But others may feel uncomfortable with a suicidal person. They may interpret his successful suicide during the course of therapy as a personal failure. They may feel guilty or responsible. They know that this can happen, so they'd rather choose not to get involved at all.[12] It's much easier to prescribe sleeping pills or tranquillizers.

It's not surprising that seventy-five percent of people who attempt suicide have seen a doctor within four months prior to the attempt.[13] The means that he often uses are the very pill which his doctor has prescribed. To help keep things in perspective we should keep in mind that, with the possible exception of Mark, most of the survivors in this book could not have made it without professional help.

The young people in this book, with the tragic exception of Peter, are survivors of suicidal states or suicidal attempts. We have no assurances that they won't resort to suicide again, especially Greta and Bill; but so far they've managed to keep their heads above the mud. They have fought hard to live. It comforts us to know that their stories have had happy endings; at least they're alive. But of course this book doesn't deal with the thousands of young people who have killed themselves. For them it is too late for happy endings.

Linda's story was placed in this chapter because her situation illustrates so dramatically the success that is possible when excellent care is combined with the will to live. She came so close to not making it. If not for the purely fortuitous intervention of a psychologist from the general hospital who just happened to spot her, she would probably have spent the rest of her life in a mental hospital. Everything in her life pointed to death and failure; her parents, the way she viewed herself, the treatment she initially received in hospital all conspired to doom her. But miraculously she survived.

To see Linda is to believe the miracle. She is tall and slender, with jet black hair, fair skin, and the bluest eyes that never look away from you as she speaks. She has the appearance and poise of a fashion model. She speaks with a strong, calm self-assurance that gives the impression that she must be very successful at whatever she does. Indeed she is. Although she is only in her early twenties she already holds an important administrative position in a large company. She has the rare combination of physical beauty, ambition, intelligence, self-confidence, and a genuine compassion for others. Linda spends her weekends working with delinquent girls who live in the inner city. Her work is voluntary.

It's impossible to imagine, looking at Linda and listening to her speak, that she is actually recounting her own story. But she's too intimately acquainted with the details of it. Every now and then there's a little tremor of emotion that gives her away. And then we recognize the old, familiar themes of self-hate, guilt, and of parents who are too absorbed by their own problems to pay attention to their children, and of death as the only solution. Then we are convinced. It's her story all right.

Why should she have succeeded when others, like Peter, who seemed to have so much more going for them, failed? We will never know. That is the enigma of life – and death.

We do know that suicide is a coping mechanism. Young people in particular resort to it because they feel that they have no other alternatives. We have to become more closely tuned in to the distress signals put out by people in trouble, and we have to be willing to take action. As the stories in this book have shown us again and again, the single greatest factor in suicide prevention or recovery is the knowledge that one person cares and says, "You matter to me. I care." Suicide can be prevented. All stories can have happy endings. But the happiest ending of all would be to have no stories to tell.

Chapter One

1   Division of Vital Statistics, U.S. Public Health Service.

2   A. Alvarez, *The Savage God* (New York: Random House, 1972), p. 42.

3   *Ibid.*, p. 54.

4   Jerry Jacobs, *Adolescent Suicide* (New York: John Wiley & Sons, 1971), p. 70.

5   Karl Meninger, *Man Against Himself* (New York: Harcourt, Brace & Co., 1938).

6   Alvarez, pp. 5-34.

7   *Ibid.*, p. 87.

Chapter Two

1   Winnipeg *Free Press*, May 27, 1977.

2   T. L. Dorpat, J. K. Jackson, and H. S. Ripley, "Broken Homes and Attempted and Committed Suicide," *Archives of General Psychiatry*, 12 (1965), 213-216.

3   Herbert Hendin, *The Age of Sensation* (New York: W. W. Norton & Co., 1975).

4   G. Zilboorg, "Considerations of Suicide with Particular Reference to that of the Young," *American Journal of Orthopsychiatry*, 7 (1937), 15-31.

5   Sigmund Freud, *Civilization and Its Discontents* (New York: W. W. Norton & Co., 1961).

6   Gisela Konopka, *The Adolescent Girl in Conflict* (Englewood Cliffs: Prentice-Hall, 1966), pp. 87-88.

Chapter Three

1   Anna Freud, "Adolescence as a Developmental Disturbance," in *Adolescence*, ed. Gerald Caplan and

Serge Lebovici (New York: Basic Books Inc., 1969), pp. 5-10.

2   Paul Osterrieth, "Adolescence: Some Psychological Aspects," in *Adolescence*, ed. Gerald Caplan and Serge Lebovici (New York: Basic Books Inc., 1969), p. 17.

3   James Anthony, "The Reactions of Adults to Adolescents and Their Behaviour," in *Adolescence*, ed. Gerald Caplan and Serge Lebovici (New York: Basic Books Inc., 1969), p. 54.

4   Adele Faber and Elaine Mazlish, *Liberated Parents, Liberated Children* (New York: Grosset & Dunlap, 1974), p. 123-125.

5   Paul Osterrieth, p. 18.

6   James M. Toolan, "Depression in Children and Adolescents," *American Journal of Orthopsychiatry*, 32 (1962), 405-415.

7   A. Alvarez, *The Savage God* (New York: Random House, 1972), p. 70.

8   *Ibid.*, pp. 113-114.

9   James Anthony, p. 63.

Chapter Four

1   Laura Z. Hobson, *Consenting Adult* (New York: Doubleday & Co., 1975).

2   Murray M. Kappelman, "When Your Teenager Needs You Most," in *Family Health* (August, 1977), p. 45.

3   E. Mansell Pattison, "Confusing Concepts about the Concept of Homosexuality," in *Psychiatry* (Nov., 1974), p. 341.

4   Calvin S. Hall, *A Primer of Freudian Psychology* (New York: The World Publishing Company, Mentor Books, 1954), p. 110.

5   Sigmund Freud, "Letter to an American Mother"

(written April, 1935) in the *American Journal of Psychiatry*, 107 (1951), pp. 786-787

6 Daniel Cappon, *Towards an Understanding of Homosexuality* (Englewood Cliffs: Prentice-Hall, Inc., 1965), p. 103.

7 Jan Loney, "Family Dynamics in Homosexual Women," in *Archives of Sexual Behaviour*, 2 (Dec., 1973), p. 348.

8 E. Mansell Pattison quoting Dr. Judd Marmor, p. 348.

9 R. Kolodny, et al., *The New England Journal of Medicine*, 285 (Nov., 1971), pp. 1170-1174.

10 Murray S. Kappelman, p. 44.

11 Z. Defries, "Pseudohomosexuality in Feminist Students," in the *American Journal of Psychiatry* (April, 1976), 400-404.

12 W. Durant, *The Story of Civilization: Caesar and Christ* (New York: Simon and Schuster, Inc., 1954).

13 P. H. Mussen, J. J. Conger, J. Kagan, *Child Development and Personality* (New York: Harper and Row, 1969), pp. 502-506.

14 Benjamin Spock, *Baby and Child Care* (New York: Pocket Books, 1972), pp. 361-362.

15 Jan Loney, p. 348.

16 William A. Schonfeld, "The Body and the Body Image in Adolescence," in *Adolescence*, ed. by Gerald Caplan and Serge Lebovici (New York: Basic Books, Inc., 1969), pp. 43 and 46.

Chapter Five

1 Eliot Asinof, *Craig and Joan* (New York: Viking Press, 1971).

2 Edwin S. Shneidman, ed. *Death and the College Student* (New York: Behavioural Publications, 1972), p. 71.

3 Robert E. Litman, "Sigmund Freud on Suicide," in

Essays in Self-Destruction, ed. Edwin S. Shneidman (New York: Science House, 1967), p. 334.

4   This is a term popularized by psychologists Edwin S. Schneidman and Norman L. Farberow to indicate that a suicide attempt, if responded to properly, does not have to end in tragedy.

5   Jerry Jacobs, *Adolescent Suicide* (New York: John Wiley and Sons, 1971), pp. 87-88.

6   Aaron T. Beck, *Depression* (Philadelphia: University of Pennsylvania Press, 1970).

7   Calvin J. Frederick and Louise Lague, "Dealing with the Crisis of Suicide," *Public Affairs Pamphlet No. 406A* (Washington: Public Affairs Pamphlets, Inc., 1972), p. 15.

8   *Ibid.*

9   Albert Camus, *The Myth of Sisyphus and Other Essays* (New York: Alfred A. Knopf, Inc., 1955), p. 4.

Chapter Six

1   Robert Jay Lifton, *Death in Life* (New York: Random House, Inc., 1967), pp. 38-39.

2   *Ibid.*, p. 492.

3   Harriet Sarnoff Schiff, *The Bereaved Parent* (New York: Crown Publishers Inc., 1977), p. 130.

4   H. Robert Blank, "Mourning," in *Death and Bereavement*, ed. Austin H. Kutscher (Springfield, Ill.: Charles C. Thomas, 1969), p. 260.

5   Erich Lindemann and Ina May Greer, "A Study of Grief: Emotional Responses to Suicide," in *Survivors of Suicide*, ed. Albert C. Cain (Springfield, Ill.: Charles C. Thomas, 1972), pp. 64-65.

6   Albert C. Cain and Irene Fast, "The Legacy of Suicide: Observations on the Pathogenic Impact of Suicide upon Marital Partners," in *Survivors of Suicide*, p. 149.

7   Alfred Herzog and H. L. Resnik, "A Clinical Study of

Parental Response to Adolescent Death by Suicide with Recommendations for Approaching the Survivors," p. 147.

8   Albert C. Cain and Irene Fast, *op. cit.*, p. 149.

9   *Ibid.*, p. 149.

10   Lindemann and Greer, *op. cit.*, pp. 67-68.

11   Harriet Sarnoff Schiff, *op. cit.*, pp. 83-99.

12   *Ibid.*, p. 41.

Chapter Seven

1   Statistics Canada. Latest figures available up to and including 1972.

2   Division of Vital Statistics, U.S. Public Health Service, up to 1974.

3   Harold Jacobziner, "Attempted Suicide in Adolescence," in the *Journal of the American Medical Association*, 191 (1965), pp. 7-11.

4   T. S. Szasz, *The Ethics of Psychoanalysis* (New York: Basic Books Inc., 1965), p. 175.

5   _____ , "The Ethics of Suicide," in *The Antioch Review* (Spring, 1971), p. 11.

6   Edwin S. Shneidmann and Philip Mandelkorn, "How to Prevent Suicide," in *The Psychology of Suicide* (New York: Science House, 1970), p. 130.

7   Aaron T. Beck, Maria Kovacs, Arlene Weissman, "Hopelessness and Suicidal Behaviour," in the *Journal of the American Medical Association* (Dec. 15, 1975), pp. 1146-1149.

8   "Suicide in Youth and What You Can Do about It," a guide for students put out by the Suicide Prevention and Crisis Centre of San Mateo County, California.

9   Stuart M. Finch and Elva Poznanski, *Adolescent Suicide* (Springfield, Ill.: Charles C. Thomas, 1971), pp. ix-x.

10   Diane Syer, Director, Crisis Intervention Unit, Toronto

East General Hospital, from a paper presented at the 9th International Congress on Suicide Prevention and Crisis Intervention, Helsinki, Finland, June, 1977, p. 2.

[11] *Ibid.*, p. 3.

[12] Robert E. Litman, "When Patients Commit Suicide," in *The American Journal of Psychotherapy*, Vol. 19, No. 4 (1965), pp. 570-576.

[13] Shneidman and Mandelkorn, *op. cit.*, p. 133.